The Educational Work of the Church

NEVIN C. HARNER

THE ABINGDON
RELIGIOUS EDUCATION TEXTS
John W. Langdale, General Editor

GUIDES TO CHRISTIAN LEADERSHIP
Paul H. Vieth, Editor

ABINGDON PRESS
NEW YORK   NASHVILLE

THE EDUCATIONAL WORK OF THE CHURCH

Copyright 1939 by Nevin C. Harner

o

SET UP, PRINTED, AND BOUND BY THE PARTHENON PRESS, AT NASHVILLE, TENNESSEE, UNITED STATES OF AMERICA

CONTENTS

CONTENTS

EDITOR'S INTRODUCTION

No one today who has given thoughtful considera-tion to the matter seriously doubts that the major purposes of religious education are necessary to the work and welfare of the Church. Certain manifestations of religious education are still under fire, to be sure. This is due in part to the inability or unwillingness of general religious workers to understand what religious education is trying to accomplish, in part to the movement's own failure to come to effective expression in methods and materials suited to the lay workers in the local church. There is no fundamental disagreement on such matters as:

That work with children is of primary importance to any church and that it should be carried on by persons who understand children and who are sensitive to the way in which lives move toward a more mature conception and expression of Christian living.

That the young people of the Church represent one of its greatest potential assets and that to guide young people in the acceptance of the Christian life and joyous service therein requires wise guidance.

That Christian living is not a status once reached, but that the adults of the Church must also be growing in mind and heart toward a more perfect expression of the Christian ideal.

That the Christian family is the most hopeful influence in the development of Christian persons, and that, therefore, parents must be given the necessary guidance so as to make their homes centers of Christian living.

That no church can accomplish lasting results

7

through professional leadership only, but that its faith and work come to expression through the service of its lay workers; that lay men and women must be inspired and taught to engage in effective service.

The time has come when general religious leaders and those responsible for the educational work in our churches need to get together in order that the contribution of each may be made available for a more effective church program. In this process the minister of the church is the key person. Few churches will rise above the interest and leadership ability of their minister. Whatever he may think of the present church school, young people's society, or other expressions of religious education, he cannot be true to his responsibility and avoid making some active effort to build a church program which is effective in its educational aspects.

If the above represents a fair estimate of the present status of religious education, the time is ripe for a comprehensive book which considers just how this ideal may be achieved in the local church. This book is herewith presented to ministers and other church workers. The author, Professor Nevin C. Harner, of the Lancaster Theological Seminary, has long been facing ministers in conferences in which the subject of discussion has been the place of religious education in the local church. In these conferences he has taken the criticism and suggestions of these ministers, as well as given them help. The results of this give and take, this study and practice, are embodied in this book.

PAUL H. VIETH.

PREFACE

THE treatment which follows in this book rests upon two convictions.

The first is that the Church greatly needs the insights and the methods of Christian education. Without these insights and methods it will be severely handicapped in its work—especially during the years immediately ahead. It is not hard to find grounds for such a conviction. To mention only one here, any churchman can call to mind congregations which are failing rapidly because of incompetency on the Christian education side of their work. These congregations have been towers of strength in years past. They have been forces to reckon with in the communities in which they are set. Their ministers and their laymen have been prominent in the councils of their respective denominations. But now they are only shadows of their former selves, and the future for them is no brighter than the present. Obviously, no single explanation is sufficient to account for such a pitiable decline, but in some instances at least the true explanation seems to be that the congregations have failed to win and hold the oncoming generation of youth. Now, to win and hold youth to the Christian enterprise is not the whole of Christian education, but it is one great part of it. For this and other weighty reasons it may be truly said that the Church sorely needs the insights and methods which the Christian education movement at its best has to offer.

The second conviction is that the minister holds a strategic place in building the insights and methods of Christian education into the life of the Church.

9

PREFACE

This is not to cast any reflection either upon faithful laymen or upon trained Directors of Religious Education. As for the former, they can make limited headway unless their ministers are sympathetic to and competent in Christian education. And as for the latter, they are so few in number that at best they can influence only a minority of larger churches. If Christian education is ever to find its way into the inner life of the Christian Church, it needs the hearty support of the ministry.

Grateful acknowledgment is due the following: Charles Scribner's Sons for permission to quote from Volume II of Philip Schaff's *History of the Christian Church;* Dr. N. F. Forsyth of the Board of Education of the Methodist Episcopal Church for permission to use my Standard for a Training Program in the Local Congregation; and the International Council of Religious Education for permission to quote from the article "Changing the Lights" by A. S. Brooks in the *International Journal of Religious Education* for September, 1931, and also from the American Standard Edition of the Revised Bible, copyright, 1929, by the International Council of Religious Education.

I am indebted to the following friends for kind permission to use reports or plans prepared by them: P. C. Shumaker, E. S. Bromer, A. N. Sayres, W. R. Yocom, J. E. Wagner, B. A. Behrens, E. L. Schlingman, H. C. Baer, Mrs. Emma N. Burkholder, Mrs. P. R. Byerly, L. C. T. Miller, D. X. Gass, Mrs. J. H. Mumper, F. I. Laucks, W. F. Kosman, W. B. DeChant, and C. G. Twombly.

It would be an endless task to attempt to enumerate all those from whom I have been privileged to learn about Christian education. The list would include my teachers, my students, the members of my family, the ministers of my denomination, writers of books and articles, and many others. I am under particular obligation to Dr. Paul H. Vieth for his kindness in reading the manuscript and offering valuable suggestions. Whatever of value the following chapters contain is the product not of one mind but of many.

N. C. H.

Lancaster, Pennsylvania.

I

WHAT IS CHRISTIAN EDUCATION?

MINISTERS of this generation have a new term to reckon with—a phrase fusing into one meaningful whole two of the greatest words in the English tongue. This term refuses to be evaded. It meets us on every hand. It stands at the masthead of conferences and conventions, and on the title pages of books. It gathers to itself committees and commissions and organizations nationwide in their scope. It lifts its head time and again from the pages of religious journals. It even peers out at us from the sacred precincts of theological seminary catalogues. It knows nothing of denominational lines or national frontiers, although its favorite domicile is the United States. It opens before already overworked pastors new doors of alleged golden opportunity, and bids them enter. Many are standing rather wistfully at the threshold, uncertain whether the Promised Land lies this way ahead or not.

The reality for which this term stands is, in part at least, very old. It is as old as religion itself. For it is of the very essence of religion to refuse to be bottled up in any one generation, but to extend its kindly sway to the children and the children's children. For many ages, presumably, this process went on from generation to generation without anyone taking thought thereto. When the first man took thought thereto— or was it a woman?—religious education in the full sense of the word was born. All that has been done since then is by way of refinement.

13

In our own day a number of factors have combined to lift this age-old process into a new and perhaps unprecedented prominence. Somewhat over a hundred and fifty years ago a greathearted printer in Gloucester, England, assembled a few ragged children in the front room of a house for instruction on Sunday. He could not possibly have foreseen that from this friendly gesture there would spring a world-wide Sunday-school movement. Wherever the Sunday school has gone it has been a most persuasive salesman of the Christian-education idea. It has accustomed people gradually to the strange notion that children have a place in the life and work of the Church. The modern Christian-education movement would have been unthinkable without the pioneer work of the Sunday school. Our chief debt to the Sunday school is not at all the methods which it has developed, but the conviction which it has kindled and fanned into a flame that the Christian Church has a responsibility to its children.

In due time the public school began to flourish, by a strange destiny, in our own country. That it did so accounts in considerable part for the further fact that the modern Christian-education movement has had its chief growth also in the United States. Through several generations our people had grown accustomed to thinking about their children, planning for them, spending for them, and lodging the hope for the future in them. It was only against such a background of ideas that the movement called Christian education could have developed.

Then around the turn of the century psychology began to move forward by leaps and bounds. Coe and Starbuck were writing their psychologies of religion. Thorndike was launching his notable series of psychological experiments. A new hope was beginning to dawn that human nature might be understood and mastered, and new tools were being forged for achieving that mastery. Now the religious-education movement began in earnest. It gathered up into itself the enthusiasm for childhood which the Sunday school and the public school had so carefully fostered, and added thereto the scientific temper and the insights and techniques which marked the new psychology.

Yet another factor entered strongly into the making of this new emphasis in church work, and, indeed, made it possible. American Protestantism has been characteristically marked by a high sense of man's responsibility. It was altogether natural that it should be so in a young and vigorous nation with ever-receding frontiers, ever-growing resources, and irrefutable evidence on every hand that man's efforts really counted. To this adolescent nation John Calvin's insistence on the sovereignty of God and the impotence of man sounded like a counsel of despair uttered by an aging civilization which had lost its grip on life. A different spirit prevailed among the pioneers of America, and it is the pioneer spirit which has characterized American Protestantism. In American Protestantism, therefore, the religious-education movement was born. It is no secret that the churchmen of England and the Continent smile rather condescendingly at our boyish "activism," and that even among us our confidence in the worth of man and his efforts has been rudely shaken since the World War. However this may be, it remains true that we have had a religious-education movement because it was our temper to square our shoulders and accept a measure of responsibility as God's colaborers. If we ever lose that temper entirely—which God forbid!—the religious-education movement will evaporate into thin air.

All of these streams of influence, and more, have contributed to the making of what many prefer to call Christian education. But now that it is upon us, there is no unanimity as to what the term means. For one person it conjures up one set of connotations; for another person an entirely different set. What, then, is Christian education?

WHAT CHRISTIAN EDUCATION IS NOT

There may be gain in clearing the ground at the outset of some widely current partial conceptions which amount almost to misconceptions. Each of the following has some basis in fact, but each by overstressing a part of the truth succeeds in the long run in obscuring the whole truth.

Christian education is not a coldly intellectual process of imparting facts. It is extremely difficult to disabuse our minds of the notion that education means primarily hurling a set of facts at the learner and making sure that they come back on the rebound in substantially the form in which they were given. Until comparatively recently this is what secular education has chiefly meant, and the natural assumption is that Christian education means something of the same sort in the religious realm. Consequently, when Christian education is spoken of, the listener begins to fill the phrase with content taken from his own childhood experiences in public school. He begins to think that what must surely be contemplated is the teaching of facts—facts about the Bible, facts about the Holy Land, facts about the life of Jesus, facts about the history of the Church. His next inevitable reaction is that, if this is what is meant, Christian education has some little value so far as it goes, but that it doesn't go nearly far enough. It does not reach the heart!

If this is what Christian education is, then, of course, there must be something more—a great deal more. But suppose that Christian education really signifies reaching the whole man! Suppose that it signifies providing for the learner in so far as we are able every type of experience needful for his Christian growth! As a matter of fact, when the International Council of Religious Education uses the word "curriculum," it makes very clear that it has in mind five types of experience—worship, study, fellowship, service, and personal commitment to Christ and His cause. Christian education is most emphatically not a coldly intellectualistic process of imparting facts.

Christian education does not imply the magnifying of teaching in the narrow sense to the neglect of the worship of the sanctuary. There are some who fear that this is what the term connotes. They dimly fear that if the Christian educators and their views should prevail, we should have many discussion groups for all ages on a Sunday morning with a feeble church service tacked on as a sort of harmless afterthought. Now, it must be admitted that in the first blush of this new movement there was a tendency to magnify the value of teaching in the narrow sense, and to hint rather bluntly that perhaps the value of the church service had been considerably overestimated. A swinging pendulum has a way of going from one side to the other. But no sane Christian educator nowadays contemplates any diminution of emphasis upon the church service, or upon worship in general. As a matter of fact, in the judgment of many the religious summer camp is the finest embodiment to date of the ideals of Christian education, and it ofttimes puts worship at the very heart of its program.

Christian education is not a man-made process of lifting ourselves into the Kingdom by our own bootstraps. This point deserves more careful consideration later, but it is convenient to treat it briefly also in this list of misconceptions. At first glance it appears that Christian education is of, by, and for man alone. It looks like something that one set of people do to another set of people independently of either God's guidance or His assistance. And, in truth, this new emphasis does say most insistently that man's responsibility is real and his efforts really efficacious. But it says much more. It can say conscientiously that in the final analysis the building of the Kingdom is God's work; that, however, this building is done in part at least through man; that man in doing his part had best take great pains to see to it that what he does is in line with what God does. If there is any one scriptural passage which serves as a charter for the Christian education movement, it is Philippians 2. 12-13: "Work out your own salvation with fear and trembling; for it is God who worketh in you both to will and to work, for his good pleasure."

Christian education is not a panacea, a cure-all, a new Messiah. Every new approach to church work is likely to be seized upon avidly, especially in difficult days. Perhaps here at last is the way out! Perhaps the adoption of a new lesson series, or the shift from the lecture to the discussion method in teaching, or the establishment of a Board of Christian Education will work wonders! The answer is, of course, that in all probability it will not. Christian education is not a trick or a device or a scheme. It is a basic method which makes heavier demands upon minister and congregation than we have yet begun to imagine.

Christian education is not what we do for children and young people as opposed to what we do for adults. It was natural that Christian education should be thought of at first as being concerned primarily with the immature members of a church. Was not secular education concerned primarily with the immature members of society? But this is rapidly being changed in both the secular and the religious realm. In the secular there is afoot an adult-education movement thoroughly grounded in the findings of Thorndike and others that adults can truly learn. In the religious realm we now see clearly that there is no age-limit for spiritual growth. Child, youth, and adult are equally the subjects of Christian education.

Christian education is not what goes on in the auxiliaries of a church as opposed to what goes on in the church proper. There is a very subtle error implicit in the title "Director of Religious Education." The implication is that when the Director is guiding the work of the church school, or the vacation school, or the young people's society, he is engaged in religious education, but that the pastor is not so engaged while he is preaching, conducting worship, or visiting the homes of his members. This inference is not fair to the pastor; neither does it do justice to the richness of meaning in the phrase "Christian education." Strictly speaking, nothing which a good pastor can do can possibly fall outside the scope of true Christian education; by the same token the term "Christian education" is as broad as the life of the church itself. What-

19

ever in it is sound must of necessity be sound not only from 9:30 to 10:30 each Sunday morning, but from 10:45 to 12:00 as well.[1] (If this seem as though the movement of Christian education is trying to usurp the whole field of church work, let the name be forgotten, but at all costs maintain the unitary character of the whole life of a Christian congregation.)

Christian education is not identical with any particular method or technique or philosophy of education. It employs methods and is guided by philosophies of education, but is not identical with them. It is more than they. In the midst of their coming and going, it abides. It is conceivable that the discussion method, the project method, the democratic philosophy of education, and all their brethren and cousins could be superseded, but what we call Christian education remain.

WHAT, THEN, IS CHRISTIAN EDUCATION?

Christian education is a reverent attempt to discover the divinely ordained process by which individuals grow toward Christlikeness, and to work with that process.

Every word in this definition is heavily laden with significance. Consider first the word "process." The bedrock assumption upon which the Christian education movement bases itself is that there is a process—an orderly process—in keeping with which personality grows. Personality-growth is never haphazard—never! We see two boys born of the same parents, living in the same home, going to the same school, associating

---

[1] It is felt necessary to stress this point here, even in face of the fact that the treatment of Christian education in this book will not presume by any means to treat all phases of a minister's work.

with the same playmates, subjected to the same Christian influences, but turning out the one a sinner and the other a saint. We are tempted to throw up our hands and take refuge in the easy statement that character-growth is a great mystery, but that is no answer. The past twenty-five years have gone far toward explaining such a phenomenon in terms of a process of unwavering orderliness. The next twenty-five years will go farther still, and the next.

Furthermore, personality-growth is never miraculous—never! It may look as though it is, but it is not. Let us face the full implications of this conviction unafraid. There are no gaps in the process which represent the sudden thrusting of God's hand into a man's life to give it a twist or a direction or a lift not in keeping with the laws of personality-growth. There are gaps in our knowledge of the process, but no gaps in the process. Why should there be? If the process is God's process from start to finish, no gaps are needed. On one occasion a speaker was endeavoring to develop this conception, basic to Christian education, of the orderliness of personality-growth. In the discussion period which followed a minister said in effect: "It is all right, of course, to try to understand human growth, but you accept, I presume, the fact of a gap between the natural man and the spiritual man which no education can bridge over." And then he quoted the oft-cited text: "The wind bloweth where it will, and thou hearest the voice thereof, but knowest not whence it cometh, and whither it goeth: so is every one that is born of the Spirit." It was on the way home that another minister remarked with true penetration that the figure of the wind does not represent disorder at all, because there is nothing in God's universe which is more obedient to law and order than the wind. The wind is indeed quiet and unassuming in its coming and its going, but it is not disorderly. Just so is every one that is born of the Spirit! To borrow one of Horace Bushnell's telling phrases, there are no miraculous and inexplicable "gales of the Spirit." There are gales of the Spirit, indeed, but even the gales obey their Master's law. The first effect of such a conviction may be to thrust God afar off and lose the sense of His immediate touch upon human life; the next effect is to bring Him "closer . . . than breathing, and nearer than hands and feet," and to fill all of life with divine significance.

Consider, then, the words "divinely ordained." It is of the utmost importance to note them clearly. It is our earnest conviction that if there is a process of personality-growth, it is not our process, but God's. We discover it little by little, but He made and ordained it. It was here centuries before there was such a thing as psychology. Now, in our own day we are tracing it out little by little. As we do so, we ought to proceed with untold reverence. We are "thinking God's thoughts after Him." We are touching the hem of His garment. There is nothing which, if truly understood, has more of a religious overtone than psychology. The psychologist as he works in his laboratory and pores over his statistical data and then announces a well-substantiated finding, ought to hold his breath in sheer awe, and then say with all reverence, "I have just succeeded in uncovering another tiny corner of God's plan for human life."

We may well turn aside at this point to note that such an outlook requires a reasonable belief in the immanence of God. It does not at all require such an overemphasis upon God's immanence as to lose His transcendence, but it does require a real immanence. If God is not in some true sense in His world, then all that has been said here falls to the ground because it has nothing to stand on. If God is indeed the "wholly Other," if He is so far above this world that He cannot be discerned in the world, if what goes on in the homes and the communities and the fellowships which dot this planet has no real part in God's will and plan, then Christian education as we have known it in America is chiefly an illusion. If Continental critics of American Christianity say that we have had a foolish over-confidence in the speed with which our own efforts can count for the Kingdom, we may well take heed and learn. It is true. If they say that we made too much of the good in human nature and too little of the awful tendencies toward sinfulness in the same human nature, that too is true. If they say that we were losing our sense of awe toward God, that too is true. We patted God condescendingly on the head and admitted Him to membership in the social group with only an occasional blackball. We had, no doubt, lost our sense of proportion. But when they begin to draw God up and out of our common life as the sun draws water away from the earth into the clouds above the earth, then in truth must we cry a halt lest our common life be reduced to a godless desert. For many, that is not the beginning but the end of true faith.

But to return to the definition: consider next the phrase "toward Christlikeness." This phrase defines the goal of the individual's growth. When we think of what we want him to become, we think of Christ. We can think of nothing finer. The individual's arrival may not be at all within the span of these threescore years and ten, but, rather, on some far-distant shore of eternity. But it is toward that goal that he presses on at seven, at seventeen, and at seventy, and it is toward that goal that we strive to help him. We may say, therefore, that Christian education derives its method from the sciences of psychology and sociology; it derives its objective and its sustaining faith from historic Christianity.

And, finally, consider the phrase "to work with that process." In all that we do in Christian education we are merely working with that process. Whether we preach, or teach, or order the life of a home wisely, or take counsel with an individual pilgrim along the Christian way in the light of the best findings of psychology, we are merely working with that process.

Perhaps instead of saying that we work with the process it would be truer to say that we allow it to work through us. The finest possible analogy to Christian education is provided by an incident which took place several years ago when the then king of England was broadcasting a speech by radio. In the midst of the broadcast a connection became loose. An humble workman in the studio took the two wire-ends in his hands, allowed his own person to become a part of the circuit, and the address continued. Did the workman create the laws which govern the operations of electricity? He did not. Did the workman create the power which carried the king's voice to the distant corners of his land? He did not. Yet through him the king's will was done. So is it with us. Whether we preach, or teach, or order the life of a home wisely, or take counsel with an individual pilgrim along the way, we are merely gap-closers in the workshop of the Almighty.

WHAT IS CHRISTIAN EDUCATION?

How Does a Person Grow Toward Christlikeness?

This, obviously, is a question of fundamental importance. The first step in Christian education is to trace out as much as we can of the answer to this question. The next step is to go to work accordingly. Many of the findings of psychology and sociology are grist for our mill as we attempt to cope with this question. It is to this same question that the three great theorists in the field of religious education have addressed themselves chiefly—namely, Bower, Soares, and Coe. Each of the three has made a notable contribution to its solution.

It may be that a good deal of psychological insight can be gathered up in nontechnical form by focusing our attention on an individual and asking what would conceivably advance him toward the Christian goal. The following is a description of a boy who is, of course, hypothetical yet real (there is no such boy but there could well be). For convenience' sake let us call him Ralph. He is, at the time he comes to our notice, nine years of age. . . . He likes very much to play, but has little or no interest in school. He is given to swearing considerably but without irreverent intent—a practice which he took up about a year ago. . . . He is fond of his father, but not on good terms with his mother. The fact is that his mother nags at him a great deal, and, furthermore, gives more of her attention to his baby sister than Ralph deems strictly necessary. The net result is that Ralph is ofttimes ugly in manner and action around the home. He has begun a rather deep-seated hatred for girls and the feminine sex in general. . . . Ralph knows little about Jesus, and cares less. Saint Paul is only a shadowy name to him. On the other hand, he cherishes a passionate admiration for one or two baseball stars who frequently make the headlines. . . . He is sublimely indifferent to the welfare of other people: the sick, the hungry, the unpopular, the dispossessed —they do not lie as yet within the orbit of his life. . . . He would turn up his boyish nose at the strange notion that "it is more blessed to give than to receive." He does not know what giving really means —whether it be to a family, a church, or a cause. . . . On the playground he plays hard and fair as a rule. In severe emergencies he will cheat a little, or lie out of responsibility for a broken window. He thinks war is glorious, and spends much of his spare time playing with soldiers. . . . He has said his prayers since he was a little boy, but can hardly be said to know what real prayer is. He generally draws pictures in the hymnal during the church service.

Such is Ralph! It is our hope as Christian educators to play a part in helping him to become a man who loves both God and his fellow men, who finds his chief satisfaction in working for the kingdom of God, and whose attitudes and actions in every major sphere of life are at least partially Christian. What can we do to help him toward that goal? If we were to take the foregoing sketch point by point and ask at each what we can do, our list might look something like the following: We might have him transferred to another school where better work is done and where a happier relationship obtains between teacher and pupils. Or—to attain the same end—we might encourage his father to help Ralph with his school work until he begins to taste success in his studies. If his swearing comes from wrong associates, we might at-

tach him to the "Cub" branch of the Boy Scout movement, where more wholesome language and activities
might prevail. . . . It would be advisable to help
his mother to change her attitude toward him. She
might accomplish wonders in Ralph's conduct about
the home by relaxing her nagging somewhat, caring
for him more as a person, and taking him to the movies
occasionally. . . . At church school we might plan
carefully to entrap his interest in a boyish study of the
life of Jesus, or of Paul, or even of Grenfell. He might
in time come to appreciate other types of heroism than
the baseball variety. . . . At Thanksgiving time we
might take him with us on a friendly and helpful visit
to a family in need, and by judicious conversation enable him for a half hour at least to put himself into
their places. . . . We might even open the way for
him to take a personal interest in that family at some
sacrifice to himself. . . . We could talk over with
him in informal fashion this thing called "cheating."
Under our guidance he would analyze it somewhat,
inquire what it leads to, what its advantages are and
its disadvantages. In the same spirit we could give
him a chance to think through what war really is, not
the war of the parade-ground but the war of the battle-
field. Perhaps he would view his toy soldiers in a
slightly different light thereafter. . . . And, finally,
we might redouble our efforts to offer him the opportunity of worshiping in a service at once beautiful and
boylike, perhaps a service in which he and his fellows
would endeavor to relate their juvenile lives to the
will of the Father in heaven.

This, of course, is a gross oversimplification of the
matter, and yet there is value in approaching the problem in this simple fashion. If, now, we review the

steps which we have proposed taking in his behalf, and restate them from his standpoint rather than from our own, we shall find them grouping themselves into a few basic types or categories. We thus arrive at a generalized statement of how a person grows in the Christian life. Freed from all technical phraseology, it might run somewhat as follows:

1. A person grows through responding to the influence of those about him. We are thinking now not of what they say to him, but of what they are in his presence—parent, teacher, minister, friend. In them he sees some way of living—good, bad, or indifferent—"drawn out in living characters," and what they are he tends to become. Furthermore, he responds to those about him not only as individuals but also as groups—the family-group, the play-group, the school-group, the church-group. These groups have their own distinctive ways of life, and these ways tend mightily to become his ways. Their hold on his life is greatly strengthened by the simple fact that they possess a virtual monopoly of something which he prizes highly—namely, social approval. They are willing to give him his share of this, if he conforms. And conform he does, as a rule.

2. A person grows through getting from life the proper amount of success and affection. Just as his body needs air and sunlight, so his personality demands the proper amount of success and affection for its best growth. The emphasis is on the word "proper" —not too much, nor yet too little. If he receives too much success, too many high grades, too much of the spotlight at the annual Easter service, too much fond praise in the home circle, too many offices, he will become a self-conscious, self-centered, self-loving personality. Some day a minister will say to him, "Love thy neighbor as thyself." If his deeper self could reply, it would say, "How I wish I could, but to save my soul I can't get beyond the narrow circle of my own self-interest." If he receives too little success, always on the sidelines, always off stage, always a wallflower, he will be equally unfitted—except after a long and painful change—for the Christian life. Some day a minister will say to him, "Seek ye first the kingdom of God." If his unconscious, habitual self could answer, it would say, "Oh, if I only could, but my time is all taken up with the pitiful attempt to get for myself a tiny place in the sun." So is it also with affection. Too much makes the person complacent, self-satisfied, overly dependent on others; too little renders him harsh and bitter or nervous and timid—a potential delinquent or a potential neurotic as the case may be. It will be a glorious day for humanity when we are as zealous to secure the proper climate for growing personalities as we now are for tomato plants.

3. A person grows through responding to the influence of those whom he has not seen. It is the prerogative of human beings alone to live in the gracious presence of "those whom not having seen we love." Across the centuries they come—Moses and Abraham, Amos and Isaiah, Saint Paul and Saint Francis, Socrates and Lao-tse, and head and shoulders above them all Jesus of Nazareth. They come to us by way of the printed page. Sometimes it is the sheer fact of their lives which impresses us most, guiding us away from the wrong into the right and inspiring us to do what we would not have dared attempt otherwise. Sometimes it is their principles and teachings, a lifetime of rich experience gathered up memorably into a few short words, from which we receive the greater help. They come to us not only through the printed page, but by word of mouth from our friends who have come to love them and now recommend them to us in sermon or church-school lesson or conversation. They come to us often most forcefully in the very lives of those about us. For almost twenty centuries now something of the spirit of Jesus has been reborn and come to life again in every good parent or good minister within the bounds of the Christian community. They come to us not only across past centuries, but across present miles of space—Kagawa, Gandhi, and Albert Schweitzer. Happy is the child who can grow up amidst the blessed company of the prophets and apostles, the martyrs and the saints of all ages!

4. *A person grows through learning how the other half of the world lives.* In some half-mysterious way which we do not altogether understand a person grows both in his love toward man and in his love toward God by learning how the other half of the world lives. Clearly, his love for his fellow man is broadened and deepened by his coming into firsthand contact with the actual life of the rich, the poor, the criminal, the recipient of charity, the diseased, the white race, the colored races. Somewhat less clearly but just as surely his love for God attains new heights through the same contacts. "For he that loveth not his brother whom he hath seen, cannot love God whom he hath not seen." It is in recognition of this mode of growth that we have our Reconciliation Tours and our Round Table Conferences. The Christian Church, on the contrary, has too largely overlooked this avenue of growth. Even its missionary program and its scattered social service contacts with the local community have

existed primarily for those on the receiving end rather than those on the giving end. We on the giving end need both missions and social service for the salvation of our own souls.

5. A person grows through losing himself in ventures of service and social reconstruction. There are people everywhere who need wise and friendly help. There are causes of social righteousness which urgently need support. In other words, this is an incomplete world in which a person's growth takes place, and its very incompleteness is his opportunity for growth. By losing himself in the "unfinished tasks of the Kingdom"—to use Coe's trenchant phrase—he stands the best possible chance of finding his true self. There is an artless, unspoiled beauty about a character which has grown not through direct cultivation but as a by-product of some worthy venture of service or social reconstruction. It is the beauty of the mother who has lived long years for her children; of the minister who has been a faithful pastor of many souls; of the social reformer whose life has been completely absorbed in some quest for righteousness. This strategy of personality-growth is distinctively Christian. It is not Buddhist, nor Confucianist, nor materialist. It is the peculiar property of the Christian Church. Have we used it to the full?

6. A person grows through thinking through his ways of living. Within limits a person can take intelligent charge of his life. Within limits he can add a cubit to his spiritual stature, if not his physical, by taking thought thereto. He can with proper help take the problems that perplex him and lift them one by one high above the level of consciousness. There in the light of his own best thought, and in the light of all of eternal truth that has come into man's ken through thousands of years he can examine them carefully and prayerfully. He can do this with problems that are primarily individual and personal, such as his relationship with his parents or his choice of a life-work. He can do this with problems that are primarily social, such as war and peace or the economic question. He can do this with problems that are primarily religious rather than ethical, such as the nature of God or of prayer. In every case he can press for a "way out" which will be in keeping with the Christian philosophy of life. Thus, his God-given intelligence enters the scene as a contributor to the good life.

7. *A person grows through taking it to the Lord in prayer.* It is difficult to find a better synonym for worship than this simple phrase from an old hymn. That is just what the worshiper does. He takes his life with its little glories and its dismal failures, as well as the life of the world in which he is set, to the Lord of all in prayer. He beseeches God to look upon it. He himself tries to view his life as God must view it; to see his little life in the light of the purposes and plans of the Eternal. He now goes beyond his fellowship with those whom he has seen as well as those whom he has not seen to a fellowship with the unseen Father of all life. There he abides for a little while. He asks and receives no miracle. But he returns in due time with a new faith, and a new hope, and a new love, because he has dwelt momentarily with Him who is love personified. Such communion is in a sense the crowning experience of Christian growth.

Granting its imperfections, we may perhaps accept this statement as a fair description of the way in which individual growth toward Christlikeness takes place in

God's world. In so far as it is a true statement, it carries weighty implications for the Christian Church and the Christian minister. Here, now, is how an individual grows. This is the divinely ordained process, as nearly as we can decipher it at the present. If so, we had better work with it. It is along these lines that we must work, if we would work at all. Here, then, is the starting-point for the drafting of a church program. If our church program exists, as we believe it does, to help Ralph and his parents and his friends toward the Christian goal of the abundant life both here and hereafter, we must construct a church program which shall take into proper account these seven avenues of Christian growth.

A Church Program in Outline

The test of a program for a Christian church is not its cleverness nor its likelihood of drawing people in large numbers nor the multiplicity of auxiliaries provided for. The true test is its loyalty on the one hand to the Christian gospel and purpose, and its fidelity on the other to the process of Christian growth. With this test fully in mind, we may visualize a program in barest outline as follows:

I. A Program Within the Walls of the Church

    a. Worship
    b. Study
    c. Service
    d. Fellowship
    e. Personal commitment to the Christian life

II. A Program Through the Homes of the Congregation

III. A Program Through a Warm, Christian Congregational Life

IV. A Program of Direct Attack Upon the Social Order

V. A Program of Extending the Christian Fellowship

We begin, of course, with the traditional program within the walls of the church. The fivefold statement utilized here is borrowed directly from the International Council of Religious Education's analysis of the curriculum. Here are five program-elements, five types of experience, five things to be done in a church. It matters not when they are done, or by what organization within the church they are done. What matters is that they all be done, be done well, and be done for all ages. What matters is that our hypothetical boy Ralph be given a chance within the church to worship truly, to study according to his peculiar needs at each successive stage of life, to give himself in service to people and to causes, to fellowship richly with those of his own age and station of life and others, and periodically to face up squarely to the Christian way and commit himself increasingly to it.

But this is not enough! It could all be done and done well, and many of the sources of his growth yet remain untouched. All the while he might be spending a good part of his life in a home which in precept and practice was a partial denial of Christianity. Or, his observation of the way the members of the congregation treated one another and the way the congregational life was ordered might more than offset what the congregation said to him through minister and teacher. Congregations too teach more by what they are than by what they say. Or, he might be prey to community influences which all the time were pulling him back from the heights to which the church was endeavoring to lure him. Hence, it seems short-sighted to say the least for a church to limit its purview to what transpires within the four walls of the church building. It can be indifferent to nothing which vitally touches the lives of its members. Hence the second, third, and fourth points in the outline above!

And, finally, there must be provision for extending the Christian fellowship to those who do not as yet belong to it. In distant lands and places this becomes missions. Closer home it becomes evangelism through the survey, through special services perhaps, but especially through the cultivation of true friendship with the unreached one by one.

It goes without saying that the chapters which follow dare not attempt to deal with all the phases of the program thus outlined. Rather they must confine themselves to Christian education in the narrower and more conventional sense of that phrase. It still remains true, however, that if the process of growth toward Christlikeness is as broad as it has been represented to be, then a full-blown program for a Christian church must be equally broad in its scope. If any of the above-named elements of a church program seem to have little or nothing to do with the unfolding lives of a church's members, let them be stricken out. If this cannot conscientiously be done, there seems to be no alternative but to allow them all to become mandatory for the Christian minister.

II

BUILDING A PROGRAM TO FIT PEOPLE

IN Christian education, as in all things, there is a first step. In Christian education, as in all things, the first step is simple, far from spectacular, and not at all what it is sometimes thought to be. What is the initial move for the church which is earnestly desirous of doing the work of Christian education? Shall it install a new series of lesson quarterlies in the church school? Or introduce handwork? Or organize a young people's society? Or renovate the church basement so that the Junior Department can meet in it? Or secure a Director of Religious Education, if the church be large?

On careful reflection it seems that the first step is none of these. It is in a way simpler than any of these, and yet perhaps far more difficult, for it consists of turning one's eyes in a certain direction and holding them there steadily despite all temptations to gaze elsewhere. *The first step in Christian education is to come to think first, last, and always of people.* In technical phraseology this is called the "life-centered principle" or the "experience-centered principle." At root, however, there is nothing technical about it, but, rather, something very homely and human. It is merely a kindly pastoral bent of the minister's soul. To see clearly and to feel deeply that a church exists for people—this is the first commandment with promise in the task of Christian education.

A CHURCH EXISTS FOR PEOPLE

The incomparable illustration of this basic insight

is the statement attributed to Dr. Campbell Morgan.[1]
On one occasion he was on the point of preaching in
a theater. The electrician had turned on the footlights
and dimmed all the others, so that Doctor Morgan
himself stood in a blaze of glory while the people to
and for whom he was about to preach were in semi-
darkness. When he arose to speak, he paused to request that the footlights be turned off and the lights
in the theater proper be turned on, and then added sig-
nificantly, with a wave of his hand toward his audience,
"My notes are out there."

How clearly and unforgettably this catches the essential truth of the matter! In symbolic fashion it
gently reminds us that a sermon exists for people. Indeed, what other justification can a sermon possibly
find for its existence? Its highest purpose is to help
people where they are; to bring the eternal gospel to
bear upon their daily lives. Yea, more, it ought to
grow out of their lives. A famous professor of homiletics used to paint before the mind's eye of his students a vivid word picture of the soul needs of some
man, real or hypothetical, and then say: "Now, prepare a sermon and preach it to that man!" That is
true Christian preaching. And—by the same token—
a church-school class, a morning church service—indeed, every last phase of a church's life exists for people. They are to the program of a church what the
sun is to our solar system—the center of gravity around
which all else revolves.

Some Objections to This Viewpoint

Before going further with this point of view,

---

[1] *International Journal of Religious Education*, September, 1931,
p. 20, "Changing the Lights," by A. S. Brooks.

that a church exists for people, it may be well to face briefly some of the objections to it which quite naturally raise their heads. They look quite plausible, and, indeed, they are. However, the truths they plead for are in no wise incompatible with this point of view, if it be held with a fine common sense.

If we think of people first, last, and always in a service of worship, shall we not thereby be minimizing God? Ought He not to be central in our worship? This objection is sure to arise in the mind of any person sensitive to truly objective worship. The simplest answer would seem to be that a journey has both a starting point and a destination. The experience of worship can fittingly be regarded as a journey of the soul. Its starting point is where people now are—in the very midst of their hopes and fears, their failures and their aspirations. How different the worship of a Thanksgiving service from that of a people whose homes have just been devastated by flood! But its destination is something other. The end of the worship pilgrimage is at the very throne of grace. It need not detract from the importance of either to say that a road has two ends.

Again, *if we think of people first, last, and always in a church-school class, shall we not be in danger of minimizing the Bible?* It would seem, in all frankness, that we are. A very wise professor once said to a group of students: "The trouble with religious education is that it has no past." He did not mean at all that the religious-education movement had existed only a short while. What he meant was that the movement has at times lacked a proper appreciation of the rootage of present life in the past history of the human family. In dealing with people today its peculiar bent makes it prone to be so preoccupied with their day-by-day experiences as to forget that through long ages people have loved and hoped and trusted and through equally long ages God has dealt graciously with mankind. To forget that marvelous story—told pre-eminently in the Bible—while trying to educate a modern child in religion is like ignoring Bach, Mendelssohn, Haydn, and Gounod in a school of music. It is like trying to grow a tree in mid-air without roots. There is, then, a real danger of falling into this error, but we need not do so. We shall—even with this point of view—use the Bible a great deal, but we shall use it when and as people need it. We shall slip its choicest passages into people's lives to meet some problems, or allay some fear, or open up some new vistas of living. We shall teach the Bible best not as a rule by teaching the Bible primarily, but by teaching people with the help of the Bible.

Again, one may ask, *does not this viewpoint relegate the Christian gospel to a secondary place?* Is not this, after all, a *Christian* church? Is that sacred adjective to be robbed of all its significance? This is not a Buddhist church, nor a Confucianist church, nor a humanist society. Its most distinctive feature is that it is the custodian of the Christian gospel. Ought not that gospel be central? When the minister rises to preach, are we right in saying that he should think first, last, and always of people? Ought he not think rather of the gospel whose messenger he is? And the answer, of course, is that in our stress upon people we have no thought whatsoever of relegating the Christian gospel to obscurity. There can still be gospel sermons a-plenty, in the best sense of that grand old term. What seems worth insisting upon is that the rich variety of the manifold gospel shall be made to minister now to one and now to another need of struggling humanity. For the most ardent proclaimer of the gospel it still remains true that his "notes are out there."

Let it stand, therefore—this principle that a church exists for people. Its errors can with care be avoided, and the truth into which it leads us is infinitely precious and greatly needed. Our contemporary world is showing itself very impatient with any branch of Christendom which forgets that it exists for people. Now as always we need the clear vision of our Lord that man was not made for the Sabbath, nor for the Bible, nor for the Church, nor for any doctrine, usage, or program. It is they which are made for him.

BUILDING A PROGRAM FOR PEOPLE

The fundamental principle in building a program for a church, then, is to construct it around the interests and needs of *a particular group of people*. No two church programs can be precisely alike, for the reason that no two congregations are precisely alike. One congregation consists predominantly of older people, another of younger; one is rural, another urban; one includes many college graduates, another few; one is rich, another poor; one is set in a community where there is ample provision for cultural needs, another is without books, music, and art. If the point of view thus far developed is at all true, a church's genuine success will depend in considerable measure upon the degree to which its program grows naturally out of the lives of its own people.

From the minister's standpoint, this process of helping his church's program to rise out of the life of his people seems to fall into three main stages.

1. Find out all one can about these people. It is possible to do this with varying degrees of thoroughness. At one end of the scale is an alert and sympathetic pastor keeping mind and heart open as he goes in and out among his people. Here, clearly, we stumble upon one of the true and abiding purposes of pastoral visitation. This time-honored practice is far from being outmoded. At the other extreme is a thoroughgoing sociological survey which would delight the soul even of a statistician. In between there are many intermediate stages.

One useful and interesting strategy was employed by Dr. Albert W. Beaven during his fruitful ministry at the Lake Avenue Baptist Church in Rochester, New York. Whenever Doctor Beaven and some of his people began to sense the existence of a need—for example, in the matter of family worship—he was more than likely to appoint a commission to ferret out the facts. Thus pastor and people together would get a true picture of the congregation's life at that point. It is little wonder that one gets the impression in reading of this church's work that it actually "counted" in the lives of its people.

Another illustration of these intermediate stages is furnished by the experience of a theological student who became the supply-pastor of a congregation during the latter part of his seminary course. Inspired by the idealism of youth, he was not content to undertake a stereotyped program, indistinguishable from that in vogue in a hundred other congregations. Accordingly, he undertook to discover more or less systematically some needs of his people upon which a program might

41

be built. His experience is richly suggestive. He studied the past history of the congregation and its present condition from a number of worth-while angles. But what concerns us more directly here is a further step which he took. Enlisting the interest of a representative group of his young people between twelve and eighteen years of age, he sounded them out on a number of salient points of Christian knowledge and conviction. His findings fairly bristle with "leads" for sermons, young people's society programs, and the work of the church in general.

These young people, eleven in number, took one of the Northwestern University tests on the life and teachings of Jesus. Their scores ranged all the way from 28 per cent to 86 per cent, with an average of 56 per cent. They revealed an unexpected ignorance of some of the most elementary facts of Jesus' life and teachings. For example, only four of them knew that it was Judas who betrayed Jesus.

They took also a test of religious thinking. Some proved to have a very naive conception of God, thinking of Him as sitting in heaven on a golden throne, or spending most of His time in watching everything we do day and night. About half of them felt that one can gain some reliable knowledge of the Almighty through dreams, thunder and lightning, earthquakes, and studying the stars.

Some thought that when a person asks God to punish a friend who has wronged him, or beseeches God to make his father buy him a radio set, he is exemplifying fair types of prayer.

Six out of eleven held it "fair" to believe that if a person belongs to the church, he will go to heaven.

Five out of eleven believed that ushering in the kingdom of God means primarily getting everyone to join the church. Only five of them saw any connection between the Kingdom and a cessation of quarrels, fights, and wars.

42

Three of them held that it matters more to God how regularly a person says his prayers than how hard he tries to live a good life.

Ten filled out a questionnaire on race relations. All of them agreed that "all people should be treated as individuals with no discrimination as to race." All but two believed that "all races have approximately equal potentialities or possibilities of development." (Obviously there is little or no race problem in this community.)

A questionnaire concerning war and peace brought results more disturbing. Of ten young people nine were convinced that it is the duty of every citizen to defend his country in times of crisis, and five went so far as to express their willingness to participate, if called upon, in any war into which this country enters.

An inquiry among a few young people revealed the deplorable fact that in none of their homes is grace at meals said regularly.

Most astounding of all was the discovery that among eight young people none knew the original meaning of the denomination's name, only one thought distinctly of Jesus as the Head of the church, none was able to name any of the governing bodies or judicatories of the denomination, none could name the four boards of the denomination, and only a few could mention any of its fields of missionary endeavor.

Here, surely, is raw material for a church program! However, such studies are not enough. It is not sufficient to assess the attitudes and convictions of the people themselves. In order to get a comprehensive picture of their true needs it is necessary to consider as well the community which forms the setting for their lives. In it they live and move and have their being. From a study of it there will arise more clues for the building of a church's program.

The following may serve as an instance of such a

study. It is based upon notes taken by a field worker for the Institute of Social and Religious Research during the Institute's survey of village communities in New York and Pennsylvania. The community in question consisted at the time of a small village with a population of 621, plus an outlying rural area with a constituency of about 1,300 more. There were then (and probably still are) eighteen churches in this community. Our present interest is in the meaning of these notes for the programs of these eighteen churches.

The village school building is a frame structure of four rooms, unprepossessing in appearance, and located in a small schoolyard which serves inadequately as a playground. There are only about forty books in the library, and there is no trace of a laboratory. The entire teaching force consists of four teachers. Of the 40 high-school students only 9 are boys. There is no school organization at the present time of any kind with the single exception of an orchestra—no athletic team and not even at present a literary society.

Outside the school system there is practically nothing in the community of an educational nature. There has never been a Chautauqua. About the only events of cultural value are the occasional plays given by the high school and the music rendered by several out-of-town bands. (And this in spite of the fact that there are eighteen churches in the community!)

There is no adequate industrial outlet for the men of the village. A factory within the town gives employment to about thirty women, and in this way renders a real service. Two miles away is an industry with room for a dozen or so men. A gristmill hires three men, and a wholesale store twelve more. Large numbers of men are forced to find their work elsewhere in mines, factories, and brickkilns. In fact, during the week there is a marked scarcity of men about the town. And yet on the edge of town there are deserted brickkilns and in the neighborhood there is good brick clay.

The chief business of the community is agriculture, which too has its problems. In the first place, the fertility of the soil is below par. In the second place, the farmers have been under the economic tyranny of a wholesale merchant in the village who exercises a virtual monopoly over the purchases of the entire community.

The tenants, who constitute 40 per cent of the farmers, find it difficult to pay the prescribed rentals and at the same time keep enough for their own living. As a consequence a number are leaving for the cities.

High taxes complete a situation which lowers the standard of living distressingly. Except in the village modern conveniences are scarcely found at all. Houses in many cases are in indifferent repair. Few books are seen in the homes. In the whole community there are only two miles of improved road, and they were financed by the state. The farmers have neither the self-confidence nor the vision of co-operation necessary to enable them to band together for their mutual benefit and protection. The logical outcome must be the gradual decline of the population of the community, a process which is going on even now. (Apparently the churches have washed their hands of the whole affair.)

The most serious deficiency in the social and recreational life of the town is its neglect of the young people. There are in the village, not to mention the outlying community, 75 young people between the ages of 14 and 20. For them no provision whatsoever is made, barring a Boy Scout troop which is nine tenths dead. The community suffers in several ways. For one thing, it has a reputation for a certain looseness of morals among its young people. For another, there is a slow exodus of youth from its borders, which must be attributed in part to this lack of social attractiveness. (Even from purely selfish motives, the churches could scarcely find more profitable employment than to organize in healthy forms the social life of these young people.)

These are but halting examples of ways in which the lights can be turned on over people. In whatever

45

manner seems most feasible it is the minister's solemn obligation to note carefully the points at which the lives of his people need rounding out and completion. He may find that they have been left in almost total ignorance of the larger program of the denomination, or that low standards of sexual morality prevail among them, or that they have had little training in either public or private worship, or that they are starved for opportunities for social fellowship, or that many of them are physically and spiritually broken by the difficulties and uncertainties of making a living. Whatever he finds will rest heavily on his heart, and will find its way inevitably into his sermons, his prayers, and the building of what (for want of a better name) we call a church program.

2. *Take stock of what the church in question is now doing.* This surely is the next step in building a church program to fit people—namely, to put alongside of what ought to be done an honest statement of what is actually being done at the present moment. This may be an humbling experience for a minister, but it is abundantly worth while. It will reveal to what extent his church is alive—fully, intelligently, devoutly alive!

There are, doubtless, many ways of doing this. Perhaps as good a way as any is what we might call a purposeful, conscientious soliloquy. We see a minister sitting down in the quiet of his own study to face a series of heart-searching questions about his church and his own work. (Later on he may wish to consider these same questions with his church-school teachers or the members of his official board, but first of all with himself!) There is before his mind's eye also a clear-cut picture of the needs of his people. The actual is now to be judged in the light of the ideal. His mind will be constantly shuttling back and forth between these two. The questions he faces may be somewhat as follows:

1. *My preaching*

What were the themes of my sermons during the past ten or twelve Sundays?

More important still—what purposes was I trying to achieve through these sermons?

Were they what my people needed most?

How many of my people did I reach through these sermons?

Did I unconsciously aim them at any one group to the neglect of another group? At the old to the neglect of the young? At the educated to the neglect of the uneducated?

Is there any evidence that my people received any help from these sermons?

If I had never preached a sermon, nor heard one preached, nor read a book on homiletics, but had fashioned my preaching with regard solely to what the people needed, how would I have preached?

2. *The services of public worship*

Let me now think over the services of the past months:

First, the liturgical elements, if any. Were they what my people needed? If I had never so much as heard of a liturgy and were setting out now to create one to meet the spiritual needs of these people, what would it be like?

Second, the Scripture lessons. How many were thoroughly meaningful to the congregation? Is it likely that the members thought back upon these readings gratefully during succeeding weeks?

Third, the hymns. Did the congregation sing the hymns as though they meant them? Did they think of what they were singing? Were these hymns the ones they needed most?

Fourth, the music of organ and choir. In what ways would the people's lives be poorer at this moment if there had been no such music?

Why do my people come to church anyhow? What does it mean to them? Is it primarily an aesthetic experience to be enjoyed? Or a chance for social fellowship? Or mere routine habit? Or is it for them authentic contact with the Eternal through which they are helped in specific ways?

If I had never heard of a service of worship and were given sixty minutes to be used as I please, how would I use it?

3. *My pastoral visitation*

How many homes did I enter during the past months?

What did I see there? Did I see all that was to be seen? Have I so disciplined myself in psychology and sociology as to be sensitive to deep-lying hungers, temptations, and anxieties which do not float lightly on the surface of life?

What help did I give them? Was it what they needed most?

Have I omitted any classes and conditions of mankind from my pastoral care?

4. *The church school*

Why do my people come to church school? What is written on their faces as they approach the doors on Sunday morning? What do they expect to get here?

Do they receive a true experience of worship here? Does my answer to this question vary at all as I think first of one age-group, and then of another?

What did they learn last Sunday? Are they any wiser, stronger, kindlier this week because they were in church school last Sunday?

Let me look over the lesson-materials for the past months in all the classes from the youngest to the oldest. What subjects have they considered? What purposes have they sought to realize in the lives of people? Were they the ones most essential? Are there any indications in these materials that we are living in the twentieth century?

As I know the teachers of the school, how many of them made good use last Sunday of our lesson materials? How many of them fitted the lessons skillfully to the needs of their respective classes?

What opportunities have the members of the school had recently for joyous fellowship with one another? Have any groups been neglected?

What opportunities have they had for fellowship with alien groups in our community—the very rich, or the very poor, or the members of another race?

What chances have they had lately for doing as well as talking or being talked to? How often has the way been opened for them to actually work for the coming of the Kingdom, and to experience the blessedness which goes therewith?

If I had never heard of such an institution as a church school and were in a position to build one from the ground up according to my people's needs and interests, what would I build?

5. *Other auxiliaries*

Perhaps a similar line of questioning is in order for each of them.

6. *In general*

What is being done by other agencies in this community? What specifically is left for us to do as a church?

Once more those needs of the people of this congregation—where and how are they being met through the program of this church?

If I were a recent arrival from Mars and had never

heard of a church, and had before me only these human needs and the eternal gospel, what would I do?

3. Lay plans for doing what ought to be done. This third step is naturally the most important of all, but at the same time the hardest of which to speak. It must be taken differently in every separate church. It may be that what we can learn chiefly from one another in this regard is something of the spirit in which the step is to be taken. There are no definite recipes which can be handed from one minister to another, as a housewife proudly copies the directions for her favorite dish and shares them with her neighbors. It is possible, however, to note some of the points in a church's life at which plans can be laid, and the forms they may conceivably take.

For example, it is rather clear how *preaching* may be planned to meet effectively the spiritual needs of people. In this people-centered manner of thinking the starting-point for a series of sermons will not be primarily the church year (unless one can have the positive assurance that the church year corresponds exactly to the true and deepest needs of people). Neither will it be a series of apt and striking topics chosen primarily because they hang together well. Nor yet a book the minister has just read, unless he is sure that the problems with which the book deals coincide exactly with the needs of his people! No, the only logical starting point for sermons which exist for people is the people themselves. Perhaps a new joy awaits us in our preaching, a new sense of our own worth as preachers, a new appreciation of the place of the pulpit in modern life, as we increasingly plan our preaching to meet the needs of our people. Here is a minister who is laboring earnestly with a group of adolescents to prepare them for full membership in the Christian Church. He finds that they are greatly perplexed concerning prayer, and reasons rightly that in all probability the adult members of the congregation share this perplexity. And so he resolves to preach on prayer. But his sermon is not a general, coldly analytical, logically complete treatise on prayer which he spins out in the recesses of his study as a spider secretes the strands of its web. He may go to his study to prepare his sermon, and he may take many books down from his shelves, but ever before him are the young people and their fathers and mothers who are standing on the very threshold of the experience of prayer, but know not quite how to enter in. As a great-hearted preacher said many years ago (and many others have repeated his words), the object of the sermon is more important than the subject. Or iere is a pastor who talks frequently with his church-school teachers, the undershepherds of the flock, concerning the problems which arise in their classes. Every now and then there will be a matter which baffles both class and teacher. It requires further treatment than the best which they can give it. In due time that problem, with the preacher's aid, gathers to itself a sermon. In ways such as these, and even through direct questioning, more and more ministers are gladly adopting the practice of seeking from their people, young and old, suggestions for sermons. Preaching thus becomes in a real sense a co-operative venture in which both pulpit and pew have a part.

Likewise, it is all too clear how plans may be laid in the *church school* for meeting the needs of people.

In some cases an entirely new curriculum may be required. The present one may have its origin at points so far removed from people themselves that it simply cannot be used well to help them. No lesson course can serve two masters. Either it is designed primarily to help people or it is not. If it is not, sooner or later it must go the way of all devices which forsake their primary purpose. In other cases what is most needed is that the teachers shall use freely the really good materials in their possession—adjusting and adapting, omitting this lesson, spending hours on that one, giving an entirely different twist to another from what the lesson-writer intended. The lesson-writer could not, by any stretch of the imagination, know the particular needs of this specific class. The teacher can, and does.

Sometimes the plans that are laid on behalf of people will require *changes in the organizational set-up* of the church. Here, for example, is an auxiliary which has long since outlived its usefulness, but with a strange tenacity it hangs on. If it no longer serves people, it had better go. We commonly feel that it is a mark of failure to let an organization die. On the contrary, it may be a mark of success. With organizations as with men, there is a time to live and a time to die. Again, it may be that as the plans unfold it will be apparent that a new auxiliary needs to be born (although the family is already quite large enough in most congregations). Or, it may be that an arm of the church will be called upon to undertake work that it has never thus far thought of doing. Whatever alterations are made, the essential thing is that the organizational scheme of the church become and remain subordinate to people.

Sometimes the plans that are laid will involve no

change whatsoever in the organization of the congregation, but merely *a clear, ringing emphasis* which will sound unmistakably through all that is done. More than one minister has been assisted to a new conception of his work by pondering the experience of a great metropolitan church which found itself harboring under one roof people of two widely different social levels. On the one hand were a number of millionaire or near-millionaire families. On the other—and at the opposite social pole—were a host of recent immigrants living close to the slums if not in them. For a number of years a central clue to the understanding of this church's life was to be found in the patient attempt of its fine-spirited pastor to bridge the gulf between these two groups, to unite them both into "one body in Christ." It was not so much that he set up new organizations, as that he held steadfastly to one high emphasis which he felt his people needed.

Whatever plans are laid, their unfolding ought to be as nearly spontaneous as possible. If a new organization springs up, it ought not to do so because of an official communication from denominational headquarters, but—like the bluegrass on Kentucky meadows —because it can't help it. This is not to say that there is no place for careful planning. Sooner or later some responsible body ought to see the life of the congregation as a whole, and lay painstaking plans in the light of that vision. But—let it be said once more—this is not to take the place of spontaneous growth nor stifle it in any way, but, rather, to foster, nurture, and guide it. To change the figure, the planning that is done ought to provide channels through which the deep life of a congregation can flow smoothly, freely, and to some purpose.

III

BRINGING ORDER OUT OF CHAOS

ONE of the first characteristics of Protestant Church life to strike the attention of an observer is the wealth of auxiliaries which have sprung up in our midst. We have the church school, the Christian Endeavor Society, the Epworth League, the time-honored Ladies' Aid, the Woman's Missionary Society, the Men's Brotherhood, Boy Scout troops, Girl Scout troops, guilds bearing the names of the several saints of the church, plus sewing circles, dramatic organizations, athletic clubs, choirs for old and young, et cetera, et cetera. The list varies considerably from denomination to denomination, for each branch of Protestantism has its own proud family of children and foster-children. Furthermore, to cap the climax, some of these such as the church school are subdivided into smaller units, each of which in turn tends to become more or less of a law unto itself. This total array presents a distinct problem to the Protestant Church as it undertakes to do the work of Christian education.

If memory serves correctly, it was William James who called attention to the contrast between a living tree and a brush pile. At all events it is a most instructive contrast. The two have much in common. They are made of the same material. They both have many branches. But there is an important difference between them. The first grew according to an inner principle or design; the second arose by a process of piling-up. As a result, the one is an organic unity;

the other is a confused heap. The one is alive; the other is dead. It is doubtful whether a poet will ever sing a song to a brush pile.

Perhaps it is not too uncharitable to suggest that the situation in our Protestant churches quite often resembles the brush pile rather than the tree. No blame attaches to anyone if this be the case. These numerous auxiliaries have sprung up in the course of several centuries. Each arose to meet a newly perceived need. Each was sponsored by devout and sincere people. Each has done much good. Each in turn—through the fault of nobody—was added rather promiscuously to the rapidly mounting pile. There was no central stem, no clear-cut guiding principle.

How different the situation today would be if there had been throughout a central controlling principle which, by dint of careful planning, eventuated in an organic whole! How different if there were visible now a sturdy trunk from which each branch derived its sustenance and to which it was subordinate! It seems we have strayed somewhat from one of the beautiful New Testament conceptions of the Christian fellowship—namely, a vine and its branches. It may be the word "chaos" is too strong to describe properly our present situation, but there can be no doubt that it is sufficiently disconcerting to demand a solution.

The Evils of Our Organizational Confusion

There is no thought of denying for a moment the great good which our many auxiliaries have done, even in their unrelated state. They have given timely recognition to special causes—missions, the education of children, and the like—which otherwise might have had no proper place in the life of the church. They have afforded to countless people the opportunity to work for the church and its purposes according to their peculiar interests and abilities. However, we now need to give kindly yet frank attention to the evils. These have been exposed by many students of the church,[1] but we cannot look at them too often.

To begin with, it is not at all surprising that with so many separate agencies *some things should be done twice or three times* for the same persons and often on the same day. The most glaring instance of this duplication is to be observed in innumerable churches each Sunday morning of the year between the hours of 9:30 and 12:00. In church school there is for young people and their elders a half-hour service of worship followed by a half-hour sermon on the day's lesson. A benediction is pronounced, the bell rings again, and there is another half-hour service of worship followed by another half-hour sermon. It is no wonder that many feel justified in going home to the carpet slippers and the funny paper at the end of the first cycle. But there are other instances also. In some churches the young people's department of the church school in the morning and the young people's society in the evening perform practically the same function for practically the same people. There is also in quite a few places a conflict of some seriousness between the young people's society program and the Sunday-evening church service. Furthermore, some faithful church women find themselves belonging to two, three, or four auxiliaries among which there is considerable duplication of purpose and program. With so many things in the

---

[1] See, for example, *The Church as a School*, by H. C. Munro. The Bethany Press, 1929, pp. 209-10.

world fairly clamoring to be done, we can ill afford to exhaust our energies in doing a few things over and over.

On the other hand—strange as it may appear—*we leave some things undone.* This is indeed surprising. It would seem that with so many auxiliaries in existence, all things needful would be attended to, but this is not the case—chiefly for lack of planning. Certain important functions go by default. For example, in congregations of moderate size it is not at all unusual for Juniors and Intermediates to go Sunday after Sunday without so much as tasting the experience of true worship. The older folks worship in church. The little children have their own departmental services of worship in church school. But the Juniors and Intermediates! They do not go to church as a rule, and because there is no separate room for them in church school they drag helplessly along in an adult service which is scarcely aware of their existence. Or, consider missionary education. In congregations without number we painstakingly cultivate the missionary enthusiasm of the girls and women, but vouchsafe to the boys and men scarcely a glance at the thrilling enterprise in which their own sex has played the major part. Then we wonder why our men show little interest in missions.

But the worst is not yet! There are also *bitter rivalries* at the heart of the church's life. The most tragic case is the rivalry between church and church school. The truth is that among the practical administrative issues which Protestantism must face, none is more serious than this one. One heavy-hearted minister was even heard to say: "My church is not one, but two— the church proper and the church school. It has in effect two ministers—myself and the church-school superintendent." But there are other rivalries as well. The Ladies' Aid Society and the Woman's Missionary Society, the Men's Brotherhood and an Adult Bible Class may find themselves playing the unlovely rôle of competitors rather than co-operators. They do not will it to be so. It is merely a price we pay for continuing a brush-pile type of organization.

This external confusion has its inevitable counterpart in the lives of the individual members in the form of *divided loyalties*. So many worthy auxiliaries claim their allegiance that they scarcely know how to apportion their time, their money, or their loyalty. Once again, the problem is particularly grave as between church school and church. There are some conscientious church members for whom the church itself, its services and its work, are a veritable home of the soul. But there are others, equally conscientious, whose restless spirits find lodging elsewhere. It is to the church school that they turn for inspiration, fellowship, and a chance to be of service. We may note in passing that in this competition for the loyalties of people the church school enjoys a decided advantage. For one thing, it is so obviously their very own. It does not belong to the minister, as the church service seems to do. It is of, by, and for laymen. Furthermore, the church school is their first love. As a rule, they come to know it and love it long before the church makes a clear bid for their allegiance. It is not easy, then, at the age of twelve or fifteen for them to renounce this old loyalty and take new vows to a new institution which seems strangely cold and unfamiliar. It is as if a boy had through long months been encouraged to court one girl, only to be urged later on to transfer his affections to her sister. Love is not like that, and neither is loyalty.

Again, under the present arrangement there is a tremendous *loss of invaluable energy*. There is a solemn lesson for the church in the old parable of the Mississippi steamboat which had such an enormous whistle that whenever it was sounded the paddle-wheels stopped turning. The average church has a strictly limited supply of competent leadership. It is questionable strategy to exhaust these few good leaders by requiring them to hold numerous offices, to none of which they can devote their best efforts.

The last evil—but not the least—is that *we fall far short at present of a clear subordination of the auxiliaries to the church proper*. The reasons for such a subordination lie much deeper than any petty jealousy on the part of the minister for his own precious prerogatives. After all, the church was here long before the auxiliaries existed, and it will probably be here long after they are gone. The church, with all its imperfections, is the abiding instrument of the Christian movement from one age to another. It should rightfully be the main trunk to which the branches are vitally attached. In practical terms, this clearly means that the official board of a church should stand at the very center of all the far-flung activities of the congregation, exercising a kindly sway over them all. But in many congregations the auxiliaries are bound to the official board by very slender threads, which have a habit of breaking on slight provocation. As a consequence, the work of the church moves forward haltingly and uncertainly—not at all like the mighty army it is supposed to resemble. On pragmatic grounds, therefore—simply because such an arrangement promises to work better—it is high time to recover the centrality of the church.

Three Ways Out

There are three chief ways out of our organizational confusion. Each has its own distinctive way of viewing the church and of proceeding to correlate its several parts. The first, in looking at the church, sees chiefly a number of *auxiliaries*. It seeks to bring these together, and unite them in joint planning for a high purpose which overarches them all. The second, in looking at the church, sees not primarily a number of organizations, but, rather, a series of *tasks* which the church must perform. It proposes to exalt one of these, the task of Christian education, and in so doing weld into one working unit all the auxiliaries that share this task. The third is blind to everything but the several *age-groups* of which the church is composed. It focuses its attention on children, young people, and adults, and requests as little organization as possible—barely enough to minister to the spiritual needs of these people. It solves the problem of multiple agencies by the simple device of scrapping all or most of them. Let us examine each in turn to see what measure of hope it contains for the future.

1. *The Congregational Council* (which sees primarily *auxiliaries*). This is by all odds the simplest plan for bringing order out of chaos. It requires merely that representatives of the several parts of a church come together to consider jointly their common task. In a very small church the Council may include the whole official board, the entire staff of church-school officers and teachers, and several leaders from

each auxiliary—plus, of course, the pastor. In a larger church a more restricted representation is in order—a committee of two or three from the official board, merely the general officers and departmental heads of the church school, the presidents of remaining auxiliaries, and the pastor. Conceivably, a Council of this sort might begin in an altogether unpretentious way. We can imagine a pastor summoning these leaders to his home "some evening next week" to consider a vacation church school, or the Every-Member Canvass, or some other venture belonging to the whole church. There will be informal fellowship, serious thought on the matter at hand, and a sample of parsonage cooking. As yet there is no mention of permanent organization. Later on the Council may settle down to officers, committees, and a quarterly meeting-night.

A leading advantage of the Congregational Council is its feasibility. Indeed, it is so feasible, so workable in widely different situations, that the constitution recently adopted by a major denomination recommends the Council-idea heartily to all the congregations within its bounds. It is so easy to start. It makes no radical departure in the structure of a church. No constitutions need to be amended; no bylaws added. It does not ask a strong and proud auxiliary to give up one iota of its precious autonomy, for the Council's functions are purely advisory. It has all the advantages and all the disadvantages of the League of Nations.

This type of clearinghouse for a church's work is sometimes called a Pastor's Cabinet, for obvious reasons. If cast into the form of a diagram, it appears somewhat as follows:

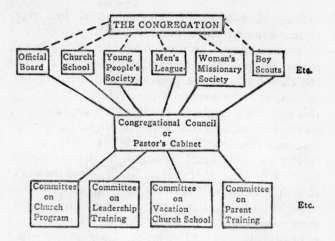

What can such a gathering do? To begin with, as already indicated, it can plan and carry through ventures which do not clearly belong to any auxiliary or any part of the church, but, rather, to the congregation as a whole. But it can go much deeper. In time, it can set itself to the basic task of studying the needs of the congregation and the needs of the community. From that day forth it enters into its rightful heritage, which is to assume the solemn responsibility for building a program to fit people. It is for this that it came into being, although it may not have known it at first. It can iron out overlappings. It can fill in ugly and dangerous gaps in the congregation's program. It can gear the program of one auxiliary into the program of another—suggesting, for example, that while the adult classes of the church school are studying the teachings of Christ, the Men's League might well consider the application of these teachings to some troublesome problems of modern life. It can even make bold,

LB
1025
C168d

LB
41
E2

once it has thoroughly tried its wings, to select some central emphasis for the entire life of a congregation over a period of several months, calling upon each organization to make its distinctive contribution to the central project.

In all its undertakings the Council has the immense advantage of being made up of the responsible heads of the several organizations. Superintendents, principals, presidents—they are all present when the Council meets. They can speak with knowledge and authority concerning the inner workings of their respective organizations. And if they (the responsible heads) commit themselves gladly to a line of action, the organizations are already half won over. To sum up, then, the Council can weld all the auxiliaries of a church into a true family with a true family spirit.

Is there anything that such a gathering cannot do? Yes, there is! Because of its very nature the Council may hesitate to face squarely the good that would accrue from having a new principal of the Primary Department, because the present principal is in all likelihood at the Council meeting. Furthermore, the Council's very closeness to the work of the auxiliaries is not an unmixed blessing. It cannot study them impartially, for it is made up of people who are caught up heart and soul in these very auxiliaries. It is too much to expect that they will view their own organizations coldly and objectively—yet such a view is sometimes needed sorely. At the risk of being ungracious, we may note one other imperfection in the Council idea. It does not subordinate the auxiliaries to the church proper. Rather, as the diagram clearly reveals, it puts official board and auxiliaries, the parent and the children, on a plane of perfect equality.

This is not good practice in a home, and it is extremely doubtful whether it is the best practice in a church.

But let us not be hypercritical! The Congregational Council is, after all, a feasible way out of a confused situation. For many churches it is at the present time the only way out. It represents a long, vigorous step in the right direction.

2. *The Board of Christian Education* (which sees primarily *tasks* to be performed). We come now to a more ambitious way of bringing order out of chaos. And yet there is nothing essentially new about the idea. It has been used for years by countless American communities—whose devotion to childhood the church may well emulate—with large success. For a Board of Christian Education is nothing more nor less than a school board in religious vestments, so to speak. A community becomes aware of its corporate responsibility to educate its children, and elects certain of its members to attend to this matter in its name. In precisely the same manner, now, a Christian congregation senses its educational responsibility, and officially commissions a chosen few of its members to discharge this sacred trust in the name of the entire fellowship.

Typically, a Board of Christian Education is made up of about seven members, with the pastor and at times the church-school superintendent as members ex officio. Some of these seven may well be persons closely identified with church school, young people's society, or missionary guild. Others are chosen primarily because of their rich experience, sound judgment, sympathetic understanding of youth, and Christian devotion—doctors, lawyers, teachers, interested parents. It seems altogether desirable that the Board be nominated by the official board, and elected by the congregation as a whole at its annual business meeting. For is not Christian education the responsibility of all the members of the congregation? If so, they alone can delegate the responsibility which is theirs. The Board, then, should be their creature, and to them it ought to report in faithful detail once a year. At its monthly meetings the Board may at first consider primarily the life and work of the church school as the chief educational agency, but it will not stop there. In time it will find itself content with nothing less than reviewing and planning for everything the congregation does by way of Christian education.

The key to an understanding of this scheme for unifying a church's life is that it views Christian education as one task among many. For each of these tasks there is, in all likelihood, an appropriate committee of the official board. But for the task of Christian education there is a glorified committee—glorified because this particular task is so important that it richly deserves to be placed in a separate category. A diagram may serve to set forth graphically the nature of this plan:

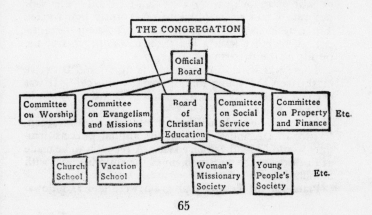

It will be noted that here at last the church proper has come into its own. The official board of the church is no longer on the same level with societies and schools, a mere *primus inter pares*. It now stands above them, as it should. One of the chief merits of the Board of Christian Education is that it manages to recover the long-lost centrality of the church.

What, now, can such a Board do? It can do all that a Congregational Council can do, and more besides! In order to visualize more clearly the possible scope of its work, it may be helpful to scan some excerpts from the minutes of a few sessions of an actual Board of Christian Education:

It was moved and seconded that "as far as the children's division's offering is concerned, the 'Benevolence' side of the envelope shall include the Building Fund; any special offering which the group desires to make shall be reported to the Board for approval." The motion carried, with the understanding that all such special projects are to be reported also at the monthly workers' conferences.

The Primary Department was instructed to extend its present program to cover a two-hour period. The new program is not to be put into effect until January 1st. Three teachers' meetings in this department were reported, together with a visitation to the parents of the pupils of the department.

There was some discussion of the question, "Is twelve or thirteen too young for joining the church?" It was decided to continue this discussion at Board meetings in the near future.

It was announced that there would be no workers' conference in December, but that the annual workers' banquet would be held January 14th. A report is to be made at this time of the measurement of the church school with Standard A.

Plans for the February program were laid as follows:

(a) Foreign Mission Day observance with a joint assembly for all ages; (b) Stewardship Essay Contest; (c) Community Training School; (d) Winter Picnic in charge of the Men's League.

The Standard A measurement, as reported at the workers' banquet, revealed the following points requiring special emphasis: (a) greater regularity and promptness of attendance; (b) training in worship; (c) more definite planning for service activities; (d) more adequate provision for social and recreational life; (e) closer relationship to the home and public school; (f) development of a plan of supervision.

The workers' conference on March 12th is to include a parent-teachers' meeting.

The vacation school committee which served last year is to meet to discuss plans for the coming season.

Some consideration was given a recommendation from the official board regarding a "Stewardship Year."

A special committee was appointed to see and invite the unchurched in the community. This committee is to make special announcements at the service on Sunday morning and at the Men's League meeting next Wednesday evening.

The church school staff for the year was elected.

Is this, then, a perfect plan? No, it suffers from two disadvantages—the one practical, the other theoretical. To consider the practical first, many congregations will find it difficult to set up a Board of Christian Education for the stubborn reason that the auxiliaries will not readily yield to its supervision. Apart from the nations of the world, there are no stancher advocates of unlimited sovereignty that some of our auxiliaries. For many years they have elected their own officers, planned their own programs, and administered their own budgets with scarcely so much as a passing nod to any higher authority. It is not easy for them now to surrender a portion of their sovereignty; and the older they are, the larger they are, and the more success they have had, the harder it is for them to submit. In some congregations, therefore, a Board of Christian Education is unthinkable for the time being. It can come, if at all, only at the close of a long process of education. In all congregations the Board will do well to claim authority very slowly, and to exercise that authority with a double measure of patience and Christian forbearance.

The other disadvantage moves in the realm of theory, but is no less real on that account. The heart of the matter is that the Board of Christian Education plan makes an unsound assumption in thinking of Christian education as one task among many which a church may perform. What, for example, of the morning service of worship? Ordinarily it lies beyond the purview of the Board of Christian Education; yet has it nothing to do with Christian education? Has it no part in the growth of persons? And what of social service? Is it, or is it not Christian education? There is, then, this theoretical difficulty in the plan we are considering. And yet, in actual life, there are congregations which have operated under a Board of Christian Education for years without subscribing for a moment to the assumption upon which it rests—which only proves once more that "life is bigger than logic."

3. *The Graded Church* (which sees primarily the *age-groups* of which a church is composed). This third plan, which bears the name, "The Graded Church," is the most striking development in Protestant church organization within the past generation. The scene of its birth and development is the Midwest principally. While a number of church leaders have

experimented with it, the names with which it is most closely bound are those of W. C. McCallum and Abbott Book.

The Graded Church has a twofold significance. On the one hand, it involves a new and different time-schedule for Sunday morning. Instead of two successive and unrelated services (church school and church), it projects two, three, or more simultaneous programs for the several age-groups, each of which is two hours or more in length and each of which is a progressive, well-ordered, and well-rounded whole. We might compare it to a series of simultaneous spiritual banquets in separate rooms. The children are in one room, the young people in another, and the adults in yet another. Each table is laden with viands designed to provide a well-balanced spiritual diet, but each in its separate room. This feature of the Graded Church is of great interest, but it is not our primary concern in this connection. It will be convenient to say more about it later.

On the other hand, the Graded Church represents a truly radical organizational plan for bringing order out of chaos. Its method of achieving this end is not to correlate existing auxiliaries, but to wipe them out of existence—leaving "a church and only a church." Indeed, this is the phrase which is most commonly used to describe it. The church school is gone. The things which the church school did are kept, but they are retained in the name of the church. Junior children study and are divided into classes as before, but throughout the two-hour period they know themselves to be attending the Junior Department of their church. The same is true of Beginners, Seniors, or Adults. But this is not all. The young people's society is no more. There may be a meeting of young people on Sunday evening which looks for all the world like a young people's society, but appearances are deceiving! This is the Young People's Department of the church holding an evening meeting for discussion and worship. All the separate women's organizations are gone likewise, or, rather, they are gathered up under a Women's Council of the church. Truly this is "a church and only a church."

Here at last is a potent spirit brooding over the deep to dispel once and for all the primordial chaos. What would a church be like in which the Graded Church principle was carried to its logical conclusion? Let us make bold to diagram a plan of organization which, in its full-blown form, has almost never been seen "on land or sea":

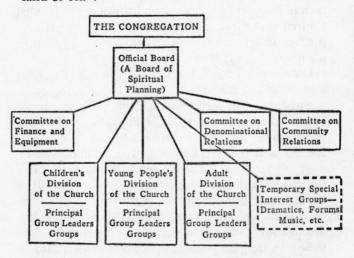

Here, at last, is true unification! There is no tying-together of auxiliaries, for there are no auxiliaries—

merely a few amorphous special interest groups which come on the stage for a brief spell and leave as quietly as they came. There is no Board of Christian Education, for there is no separation between Christian education and anything else. The whole church is organized to do the work of Christian education in the broad sense of the term. The official board is properly, now, a Board of Christian Education. That is its central significance. To be sure, it has a few committees on the side, as it were—to handle matters of finance and equipment on the one hand, and on the other to serve as bridges between this congregation and the needs of denomination and community. However, even the findings and the plans of these committees will be given an educational turn. That is to say, matters of finance and equipment will be handled by the official board with one eye fixed upon the spiritual unfolding of childhood, youth, and age within the congregation; likewise with the handling of denominational programs and community needs.

What shall we say concerning this? Granted that its earliest possible realization is far in the future, should we welcome it at all?

It would be no great tragedy for the church school merely to give up its separate existence, but it would be a major tragedy if anything sound for which the church school has stood should be allowed to disappear with it! Furthermore, it will be little short of tragic if we forget that the church school has been the greatest laymen's movement the church has ever known. This fact has been in part a weakness, but in part also a tower of strength. Through no other organization have the rank and file of church people experienced such a release of their energy and devotion! If at any time in the future the church school ceases to exist as a separate organization, then we must redouble our efforts to retain small groups for fellowship and study, and to foster the feeling that the church belongs to the laity as well as to the clergy—in a word, to keep both the form and the spirit of democracy—or our loss will be great!

And what of the other auxiliaries? Will they be done away entirely? It is by no means clear that this is the consummation we desire. Perhaps these auxiliaries have more than the temporary function of holding an interest high until the church itself takes it up. Perhaps they have the further important function of providing for diversity in unity—"diversities of gifts but the same spirit." Not all people are equally interested in foreign missions, and there seems to be no good reason why they should be. Why not, therefore, let those whose interest is deepest band together for the expression and further cultivation of that interest? The same is true with dramatics, and music, and others. It may be, then, that some auxiliaries will continue to exist for the same reason that denominations continue to exist, or learned societies, or the countless organizations in any community whose variety is a sign of the infinite variety of human nature. The auxiliaries should certainly be fewer than they are. They should not be allowed to congeal and harden. They should be kept parts of a united whole —members of one body. But it is not clear that they should go altogether.

It may well be that, observing these cautions, we can look to the Graded Church to furnish the major pattern for the organization of the typical Protestant church the day after tomorrow.

ONE MORE PROBLEM:
CHURCH SCHOOL VS. CHURCH SERVICE

It would not do at all to leave this discussion of chaos without glancing for a moment at the one spot where the confusion is thickest and darkest—namely, the overlapping and rivalry between the church school and the church service. Perhaps a backward look into history will serve best to set the problem before us. The Sunday school was begun approximately two centuries and a half after the Protestant Reformation. During those intervening years the forms of Protestant worship had sufficient time to crystallize into fairly definite shape in the several communions. Then something momentous occurred! Without warning there was set down alongside the traditional morning service a second service—that of the Sunday school. This did not happen altogether in the twinkling of an eye. At first the Sunday school comprised no measurable threat to the church service. For one thing, it began with children only, who probably would not attend church at any rate. Besides, it did not at first stress worship, but merely classes for study. Hence there could be as yet no conflict. But in time the Sunday school reached out to include adults (the chief attendants at the church service), and it broadened its program to make much room for worship (one of the chief functions of the church service from time immemorial). Now the conflict was on in earnest, and it has never been settled.

The two chief solutions proposed at this moment are the Graded Church and the Unified Service. There is no need to describe them here, because excellent literature is available on them both. Each has its own dangers. The Graded Church is likely to stratify the congregation into age-groups which never meet (in the church militant, at least) with serious consequences to the sense of congregational unity. The Unified Service may entrap children and young people into a church service which is not at all designed for them, nor even modified because of their presence. If this be the case, all that may be accomplished is that their bodies are brought into a holy place, and there is little gain in that.

It is easier to see the lines along which a solution must move than it is to suggest the final form the solution will take. It is clear, for example, that in the final settlement there must be no tiresome repetition of experience during the hours spent at church on Sunday morning. There are three types of experience which all people of full church membership age need on a Sunday morning—once and only once. First, they need a reverent, beautiful season of worship. It makes little difference where they get it, so long as they get it well. Secondly, they need a thoughtful, well-phrased proclamation of some phase of Christian truth. Thirdly, they need membership in small, congenial groups both for fellowship and for hearty discussion and study. Each of these is indispensable. These three are the protein, fat, and carbohydrate of the diet of the soul. But they are needed only once in one morning. It seems desirable, also, to keep as large a part of the church family (from the eldest to the youngest) together for the morning worship as we well can. On the other hand, we dare not drag any age-group into a service of any sort which is for them meaningless and unreal.

Putting together all these considerations, and assuming for the time being that small children should not be expected to attend the church service regularly (a later chapter will attempt to deal with this troublesome point), we begin to discern faintly the outlines of a plan which seems to move in the right direction with a minimum of disturbing changes.

For all under 14 (the age of full church membership in many churches)

1. A great deal made of worship in church school.
2. In due time an extended two-hour church school session under competent guidance. (By dint of a few necessary changes in name and church organization, this becomes readily part of a Graded Church.)
3. Five or six times a year bring all the children into the morning church service. (There are times when their presence is almost demanded by the nature of the occasion, and when the service can with least difficulty be made meaningful to them —for example, Children's Day, Mother's Day, Thanksgiving Sunday, etc.)

For all over 14

1. Very little made of worship in church school— merely a ten-minute devotional period to shake off the dust of the street and acquire the proper mood for study. (The point is that we want to make it impossible for people of this age to feel that they have had anything like a full-blown worship experience before the church service begins. This provision has the further advantage of leaving a good forty-five minutes for the class period, a part of which might be used for supervised study.)
2. No benediction at the close of church school, nor anything that sounds remotely like a benediction.
3. A careful and consistent attempt around the age of fourteen to foster the habit of regular church

attendance. (More will be said of this and the succeeding points in subsequent chapters.)

4. Adolescents given as much part in the church service as possible—singing in the choir, ushering, etc.
5. Adolescents definitely considered in planning the service.
6. Adolescents definitely considered in preparing the sermon.

This is not proposed as a final solution, but merely as a small beginning on a crucial problem. A glaring defect in the Sunday-morning services of the church is truly a serious matter. It is these very services which offer the average church its chief contact with people. If it succeeds here, it succeeds at a major point. If it fails here, it fails greatly. That is why it is so important that we act to solve this problem, and that we act wisely and soon!

IV

WHY BOTHER WITH THE CHILDREN?

ONE of the bedrock assumptions of the Christian education movement is that the church should concern itself actively and directly with the children, the immature members of the Christian community. This is an altogether familiar assumption in our own day. It underlies not only much of our church work but our public-school system as well, not to mention the large-scale propagandizing done by both Communism and Fascism. We greet it easily, like an old friend who has been with us always. As a matter of sober fact, it is an assumption which has not been generally made throughout the long history of the Christian Church.

THE CHURCH AND THE CHILDREN IN THE PAST

The Church's attitude toward children in the past has been strangely ambiguous. On the one hand it has loved them sincerely, following the clear example of our Lord. It has bettered their station in every land whose shores it has touched. It has earnestly desired them for its membership, opening the doors of baptism and confirmation wide in order that they might enter. Except during the very early years of its history and the chief periods of missionary expansion, it has recruited its ranks primarily from among them. And yet it has made remarkably little real provision for them in its midst. Very infrequently has it spoken their language, or thought their thoughts, or adapted itself in any particular to their childish minds and tiny bodies.

It is a commonplace that during the greater part of the Church's history there has been no separate institution or organization for the children. We know the exceptions which serve to prove the rule. The first great venture of the Church in Christian education was made through the instrumentality of the catechetical schools which flourished during the early centuries and declined from the fifth and sixth centuries on. But we must be on our guard lest we read into these primitive institutions a meaning derived from our own experience. As a matter of fact, they were more akin to a theological seminary of our day than they were to catechetical instruction as we know it in the Lutheran, Reformed, and Protestant Episcopal Churches. They were not designed for children primarily, but, rather, for full-grown seekers for admittance to the Christian fellowship. They had their heyday during the years when the recruits to the new faith were principally youths and adults. They broke down about the very time that infant baptism was becoming common, and in part for that very reason.[1] It is clear as can be, therefore, that they are not to be thought of as agencies for the religious instruction of children primarily.

During the Middle Ages the Church was the chief sponsor of what little education there was. Monasteries and cathedrals from time to time conducted schools. The Benedictine Rule commanded the members of that famous order to include the training of

[1] *The Encyclopedia of Sunday Schools and Religious Education.* Thomas Nelson & Sons, 1915, Vol. III, pp. 868ff.; article, "The Reformation and Religious Education," by W. W. Rockwell.

children among their duties.[2] However, such education was by no means universal. Its main intent was merely to train the official leadership of the Church. For the average child who was destined to become neither priest, monk, nor choirsinger, the Church had little concern. The Middle Ages were dark in their regard for childhood, as well as in other respects.

With the Reformation the Church entered upon a new day in its dealings with its children. Indeed, to Martin Luther, that common-sense man of the people, we are indebted for as fine a recognition of the true significance of education—secular and religious—as has emerged in any age. In rapid succession there were written catechisms representing the Lutheran, the Reformed, and the English branches of the Reformation. Once more the ancient practice of catechetical instruction was in full flower, but this time with definite provision for the young. Indeed, an organization was effected in England, the "Society for the Promotion of Christian Knowledge," whose major purpose was to carry catechization to poor children who would otherwise be neglected.[3] And, finally, at long last, the Sunday school was founded in 1780—a bare century and a half ago. A hundred years later still, in 1881, the Christian Endeavor movement was begun, followed by the Epworth League and other denominational organizations for young people. And this is the story of separate institutions for childhood, practically in its entirety! This is about all that can be said in this regard for a period nineteen centuries long.

[2] Schaff, P., *History of the Christian Church.* Charles Scribner's Sons, 1889, Vol. V, Pt. I (by D. S. Schaff), p. 535.

[3] Brown, A. A., *A History of Religious Education in Recent Times.* The Abingdon Press, 1923, p. 31.

It is equally to the point to inquire what provision was made for children in the stated services of the Church through all these centuries. There can be no doubt that they were welcomed and even expected to attend from the early days of the Christian era. By the time of the second century infant baptism was already accepted, although not generally. This meant, of course, that these baptized children were admitted even to the Eucharist, the innermost sanctuary of Christian worship. There is good authority for believing that they were actually present and participated.[4] If now we skip a number of centuries and take up the story in Germany after the invention of printing, we find evidence of a like expectation that children as well as their elders will attend the church services. At that time and place there appeared a number of devotional manuals with such intriguing titles as *The Soul's Guide, Path to Heaven, The Soul's Vegetable Garden,* and the like. These homely booklets, among other things, impressed solemnly upon parents the duty of taking their children with them to church.[5] We may safely say, therefore, that the Christian Church has quite generally wanted its children to attend church. During the Middle Ages they may even have taken part in the conduct of the liturgy.[6]

In the face of this widespread desire to have children in attendance at the stated worship services we might dare to hope that the Church would make some adaptation of those services in order to fit them to

[4] Rainy, R., *The Ancient Catholic Church.* Charles Scribner's Sons, 1902, pp. 231 and 234.

[5] Schaff, P., *op. cit.,* Vol. V, Pt. II (by D. S. Schaff), pp. 730ff.

[6] Jones, M. A., *The Church and the Children.* Cokesbury Press, 1935, p. 196.

children. If so, we are doomed to disappointment, for surprisingly little was done. No doubt sermons were, on occasion, adjusted to the presence of children. Martin Luther, for example, had the great good sense to ignore the learned in his congregations, and address himself primarily to the common people, including the children.[7] Others have done likewise, but probably many more have not. We have record of a sermon preached during the second century. Doctor Schaff describes the efforts of this ancient preacher in telling phrases: "He addresses the hearers as 'brothers' and 'sisters,' and read from manuscript. The homily has no literary value, and betrays confusion and intellectual poverty, but is inspired by moral earnestness and triumphant faith. It closes with this doxology: 'To the only God invisible, the Father of truth, who sent forth unto us the Saviour and Prince of immortality, through whom also He made manifest unto us the truth and the heavenly life, to Him be the glory forever and ever. Amen.' "[8] In Latin or Greek, German or English, preaching of that sort can mean little to children! To turn to the service itself, it is possible to examine a prayer which was probably used more than once in the early Church. It is preserved as a part of the Epistle of Clement to the Corinthians. A reading of the first sentence will suffice to show that it is scarcely calculated to wing the spirits of children toward the throne of grace. "Grant unto us, Lord, that we may set our hope on Thy Name which is the primal source of all creation, and open the eyes of our hearts, that we may know Thee, who alone abidest Highest in the highest, Holy in the holy; who

[7] Schaff, P., *op. cit.*, Vol. VI, Second Edition, Revised, p. 491.
[8] *Ibid.*, Vol. II, Fifth Edition, Revised, p. 225.

layest low the insolence of the proud; who scatterest the imaginings of nations; who settest the lowly on high, and bringest the lofty low; who makest rich and makest poor, who killest and makest alive; who alone art the Benefactor of spirits and the God of all flesh; who lookest into the abysses, who scannest the works of man; the Succor of them that are in peril, the Saviour of them that are in despair; the Creator and Overseer of every spirit; who multipliest the nations upon earth, and hast chosen out from all men those that love Thee through Jesus Christ, Thy beloved Son, through whom Thou didst instruct us, didst sanctify us, didst honor us."[9]

Perhaps the Church could not have done otherwise than it did. No religious movement, whether Mohammedanism or Zoroastrianism or Shinto, appears to have made any effort to adapt its words or its ritual to children. Neither has any other long-continuing movement, such as the Masonic order. All alike seem to have relied solely upon the powerful impact of community life upon each new generation in turn, plus a careful initiation of young adults into full membership and participation at the proper time. Christianity is by no means alone in this respect.

And yet the facts remain as they have been stated with all their tragic implications. There have been occasional prophetic voices, such as that of the French theologian, John Gerson, who in the century before Columbus proclaimed that it is with the little ones (*parvulis*) that the reconstruction of the Church must begin,[10] but far too little heed has been paid to this insight. Through the greater part of its history the

---

[9] *Ibid.*, pp. 228-9.
[10] *Ibid.*, Vol. V, Pt. II (by D. S. Schaff), p. 734.

Church has had no separate organization for children; through the greater part of its history it has made no provision for them in its services; through the greater part of its history it has made no place for them in its buildings. What a pity that such a statement is possible!

WHY BOTHER WITH THEM NOW?

The all-important question is not, What has been done in the past? but, What should be done in the present and future? Ought the church concern itself deeply with its children? And, if so, why? Perhaps a series of word pictures can be used to suggest an answer.

The first is based upon an actual experience. A young Director of Religious Education was charged with the task of setting up a vacation church school in which his own and a sister congregation would unite. In the course of his preparation he paid a visit to the pastor of the sister church to find out how many children from his parish would be in attendance. The answer came, "About six or eight." Thinking that he had misunderstood he repeated the question, and received the same reply. He was at a loss to understand these strange figures, until the pastor said, rather sadly, "To tell the truth we haven't many children in our church." It requires no prophetic gifts to foretell the future of that congregation. Barring the establishment of some new industry in the community, it has no future.

It is becoming threadbare to affirm solemnly that the children of today are the Church of tomorrow, but the simple truth is that there is a brand-new cogency today in this old argument. There was a time when the Church could neglect its own children with some fair measure of impunity, because there were always other sources from which to recruit. There was, perhaps, a new tide of immigrants from the Old World upon which to draw, or else some wide un-churched counties in the pioneer West which beckoned alluringly. But now—to turn a slang phrase to good account—"those days are gone forever." The tide of immigration has dwindled to a mere trickle. The frontiers have been pushed back to the very beaches of the two oceans, and the intervening territory thoroughly occupied by churches as well as by people. And, to carry the point still further, with a steadily declining birth rate there are not as many children as there once were in America. We cannot play fast and loose with them, knowing that if we lose three or four to the church there are three or four more in the same family whom we may get—by the law of averages. The sober truth is that we are settling down to become a nation with fixed frontiers and a rapidly stabilizing population, and woe betide the Church if it does not plan accordingly! Our situation is that of a farmer who once had unlimited acres to farm in as prodigal a manner as he chose, but now finds himself compelled to make the most of ten or fifty acres. We must cultivate intensively what we have.

At the 1936 meeting of the Association of Statisticians of American Religious Bodies, Mr. Charles J. McCollough, who is associated with Roger W. Babson, reported that during the years 1931 to 1935 church attendance had almost held its own (a loss of merely 1 per cent), but that church-school attendance during the same years had declined 8 per cent

—a loss of one twelfth in four years.[11] And then, as though to make sure that the moral of the tale was clear, he went on to point out that four fifths of all contributions to the Church are made by people over fifty years of age. It seems almost impossible to miss the point. *The Church must concern itself with children out of sheer desire for self-preservation.* In fear for her own future she is driven back to an ancient command: "Hear, O Israel: Jehovah our God is one Jehovah: and thou shalt love Jehovah thy God with all thy heart, and with all thy soul, and with all thy might. And these words, which I command thee this day, shall be upon thy heart; and thou shalt teach them diligently unto thy children, and shalt talk of them when thou sittest in thy house, and when thou walkest by the way, and when thou liest down, and when thou risest up."

The second word picture embodies a more compelling reason still—one that lies close to the heart of all true parents, teachers, and Christian ministers. Let any minister beckon before him in imagination all the children and young people of his congregation—babes in arms, curly-headed youngsters, mischievous bright-faced boys and girls, young men and maidens full of the promise of manhood and womanhood. Let him then call to mind all the personal moral problems which confront these children and young people now and await them in the future. Let him visualize some comparatively new arrivals in our national life—the automobile, the dance-hall, the movie, the cocktail bar. Let him remind himself how movie and radio, Sunday paper and city street will dangle before the

[11] Reported in *The Messenger* of the Evangelical and Reformed Church, May 21, 1936, p. 4.

eyes of these children—his children—every imaginable way of life without once bothering to label this good or that bad. Then, if he will, let him recall the striking fact that at the very moment in history when children most urgently need guidance they are being most rapidly bereft of such guidance by dint of the weakening of family ties and the abandonment of old moral and religious sanctions. By a strange twist of fate they must take their first swimming lesson during a storm at sea. But this is not all! If the minister be still in the mood, let him visualize also the social problems which these same children and young people may have to meet before their lives are finished. What international conflicts will they have to live through and face, if strength be given them, in the Christian manner? What far-reaching choices will they have to make between Communism and Fascism, Socialism and Capitalism?

Twenty-five years ago it did not make so much difference whether the Church did its task of Christian education well or not. It made some difference, to be sure, but life was considerably simpler then. The movie, the automobile, the radio were at most mere infants. The ties of family and neighborhood were stronger. There were still some absolute standards of right and wrong by which one could chart his life. The World War was still in the future with its awful train of consequences. In that day a church-school teacher could take his class indifferently through the lesson of the day, and the Church could wink at its task as educator, and the damage was not quite irreparable. But today is another day! Unless the Church makes earnest with its task of helping its children to cultivate within their own souls some abiding

Christian insights and skills with which to meet life, it stands convicted before the bar of its own conscience —and perhaps before an even greater judgment seat. *The Church, then, must concern itself with children, because even more than formerly they need the spiritual guidance which it has to offer.*

The third picture is also a creature of the imagination. Let a minister call before his chancel imaginatively six children of his congregation, and as many adults. Suppose now that he has one hour to spend on behalf of, say, world peace—with which group will he spend it? There is much to be said on both sides. As he looks at the adults, he is impressed by the fact that they will comprehend much more of what he might say in an hour than would the children. (He cannot escape, however, the suspicion that they might have much more difficulty in incorporating into their lives what they comprehend with their intellects.) Besides, these adults are people of influence in their homes, the community, the church. A change effected in them might be tripled or quadrupled in value before the accounts were all in. But on the other hand, there stand the children with all the unspoiled plasticity of child life! Impressions made on them will be easily made, deeply made, and everlasting. He might call to mind (if he had seen it, as some of us have) a leaf of feather-weight falling upon a newly laid concrete pavement while it was still moist and soft to the touch. With a minimum of time and effort it left there indelibly the leaf-pattern, complete in every rib and marking. Twenty-four hours later it would have required hours of labor and the skill of a sculptor to produce a like effect.

In actual life neither minister nor church has to

make a clear choice between the one and the other. Within limits both can be done. And yet, after all, there are only so many hours of time available, and so many dollars of money for doing the work of the church. How shall they be spent best? There is much to favor the view that a considerable proportion of them—probably much larger than is usually the case—might well be devoted to the children. *The Church, then, must concern itself with children in order to make its resources count for the most.* It must do this in the sacred name of efficiency.

A fourth picture is also imaginative, but based on reality. Let the minister now focus his attention on the technical perfection of all that surrounds his children during the week from the movie to the latest automobile. Above all let him think of the modern public school with its attractive classrooms, its scientifically designed seats, its maps, pictures, and globes, its varied activities, its fascinating textbooks, and its well-trained teachers. All week long these children spend a greater part of their waking hours in such an environment. And then on Sunday morning they come trooping into church school. What do they find there? How do the rooms compare with what they are accustomed to during the week? The maps? The blackboards? The lesson quarterlies? The teachers? What conclusions will the children draw? Will they decide that religion is as important by all indications as arithmetic, or will they make the opposite deduction that apparently religion belongs to those marginal affairs which can be handled any old way because they are of such little importance?

Whether we like it or not, the competition that the church has to meet today is infinitely stiffer than formerly. Ever so often someone complains that the modern church school in spite of its improvements is failing to hold the children as well as the old-time Sunday school did. The truth is that the only salvation of the old-time Sunday school was the lack of competition. It would get nowhere today. Children and young people would walk out of it in droves. *The Church, therefore, must concern itself with children and a proper provision for them in order that it may not lose caste in their eyes.*

The fifth and final picture is a true one. It has to do with a visit to the home of a college professor and his family. The home was an attractive one, well situated with a spacious lawn and pleasant shrubbery. As the visitor made his way to the door he made mental notes of these features. Upon knocking, he was admitted to the living room and suddenly found himself stumbling over and walking around a varied assortment of children's toys. His first reaction was to protest inwardly against such a state of affairs, and to regard it as incongruous—to say the least—with the outer appearance of the home. But the more he thought about it, the more reconciled he became to it. Perhaps this was just as it should be! After all, does not a home exist in a real sense for children? Biologically, religiously, from almost any standpoint that would seem to be so. Do we not say time and again that children make a home? Their presence creates the home spirit. Their presence draws out from parents the best that is in them. What more natural than that the children should occupy the center of the home, and that the life of the home should center in them?

May it not be that this way of thinking holds with

equal truth for a church? There is no finer way to think of a church than as a family, made up of young and old and bound together by a common heritage and a common purpose. Perhaps a church exists in a real sense for its children, to hand on to them undimmed the heritage which it has received from its fathers. Perhaps, moreover, children make a church. Perhaps their presence can draw out from the members of a congregation the best that is in them, and actually create a finer church spirit. It may well be that more than one congregation would find a new lease on spiritual life if it were to gather around its own children and devote itself unsparingly to their Christian nurture. We hear it said frequently that the home church needs missions not for the sake of Japan or China but for its own sake, and that is abundantly true. A church needs some cause into which it can throw itself recklessly, in order that it may thereby find its own life. But here at its very fingertips is just such a cause splendidly made to order for such a purpose! Here are children and young people with lives to be guided, characters to be built, energies to be released, and holding a peculiar claim upon the affections of the congregation. It may be that Christian education holds the key to a new life for every church that is willing to make the venture of love which it entails. *The Church needs to concern itself with its children for the sake of its own soul.*

All these lines of thought converge upon a conviction whose truth it is difficult to escape. In order to keep it true it is not necessary to push it to the point of implying that all else besides work with children—missions, social service, the spiritual care of adults—is worthless. All that these foregoing considerations demand is that a church, every church, concern itself with its children more than the Church universal has done in the past and more than most churches are doing in the living present. In a world where Communism and Fascism are leaving no stone unturned to indoctrinate the new generation with their distinctive tenets, how dare the Church neglect its children? How long will the children of the world be wiser than the children of light?

A Few Inevitable Implications

If this conviction be true—that the church has a well-defined responsibility to its children—then certain implications follow inescapably.

The first is for the minister. For him as the official leader of a congregation this conviction involves a rethinking of his task, a reallocation of his time, and perhaps the cultivation of some abilities hitherto neglected. It is revealing to read an actual account of his work written by a minister who, without becoming a faddist or neglecting other phases of his ministry, has yet seen clearly his obligation to childhood and youth.

The question of how much of my own time I devote directly or indirectly to work with children and young people is very difficult to answer, either in terms of percentage of time or total hours, perhaps because my work is not blocked out systematically enough on a schedule that could easily be checked and measured. I can best phrase an answer by telling what I do for children and young people. Of course I teach the catechetical class, which up to the present year has been meeting one hour each Sunday afternoon from New Year to Easter. I conduct a special children's church once each month during the second half-hour of the church-school session for Primary, Junior, and Intermediate pupils, said service taking the place of the departmental worship services for the day. I am responsible for all teacher-training work, which has been done in several ways. I have conducted over a three-year period a class in the International Standard Course. I have subsequently taught occasional teacher-training classes in isolated courses since that time. I have kept close to the superintendent and departmental superintendents, and to individual teachers. During the past year in particular I have acted as a real supervisor, sitting in at class sessions and subsequently conferring with teachers on their methods, or teaching the class as a sort of demonstration in the presence of the teacher. I have also conducted departmental workers' conferences for the purpose of introducing the lesson materials at the beginning of each quarter. During one year I served as a regular teacher in the Junior Department; another year I did the same in the Intermediate Department. Another year I was adult counselor to our young people's group which was meeting that year on Sunday evenings at 6:40. I have done occasional teaching for the men's class, but outside of the two years above specified I have never been tied up to any class but have visited around in all departments as substitute teacher, supervisor, or participant in the worship services. Almost every year I have been principal of the vacation school which runs for five weeks, at the same time acting as a teacher in the Junior Department. I have also been chairman of the vacation school committee. In other words, teacher-training and vacation school have been my special prerogative all through my pastorate here. Recently (two years now) I have consulted rather constantly with the leader of our parent-training class. I am ex officio a member of the church-school cabinet which meets monthly, and thus give some time to the administration of the school. Odd bits of time are also given on such occasions as special Boy Scout events and the like.

The minister here speaking is pastor of a congregation of almost nine hundred members, with the usual amount of preaching and pastoral work to attend to. In addition, he has rendered yeoman service to his denomination. An interest in childhood and youth is not incompatible, apparently, with any other worthy interest in a minister's life. It may indeed crowd out some trivial interests, as it ought to.

A second implication is for the congregation. This conviction which we have been considering may require a group of Christian people to rethink their task and reshape their organization. First of all, it compels them to face squarely the fact that the children of the church and the responsibility for their Christian nurture belong to the entire congregation. To whom else would the responsibility belong? These children are not the pastor's children. They are not the children of the church-school teachers and officers. Those faithful servants carry no whit more responsibility for childhood than does any other member of the congregation, except as the whole fellowship delegates that trust to them. These children do not even belong exclusively to their own parents. In the sacrament of baptism (or its equivalent) the living fellowship of the church claimed each child in turn, and at the same time assumed a measure of responsibility for his nurture in the faith. No, these children and their Christian upbringing are in a real sense a charge upon the entire congregation.

The next step is to fashion a form of organization which will give practical expression to this corporate responsibility. The need for such a step is great, for the reason that we find ourselves in a most anomalous situation throughout the greater part of Protestantism. The strange truth is that a person in joining the average church does not obligate himself definitely for the children of that church. As a member of a community

—whether he has children of his own or not—he must help to educate the children of the community, and the law will remind him none too delicately of his obligation if he tries to evade it. But his church membership entails no such responsibility.

A bit of statistics will serve well to clarify the point. Of a church membership of 150,000 in a certain synod of an American Protestant denomination, only 44 per cent are members also of the church school. What does this mean? It means that less than half of the members of this synod pay the bills of the church school (except as parents who are nonmembers support the school through their children's offerings); less than half constitute the group from which the officers and teachers are chosen; less than half elect the officers and determine the policies of the school. But we have not yet exhausted its meaning. In view of the fact that the church school is the chief agency for Christian education within the synod it means that less than half assume any obligation for the spiritual nurture of the synod's children, and, conversely, more than half wash their hands of all such responsibility. This, of course, is not quite true. The nonchurch-school members help to provide coal, light, janitor service, and the time of a minister—all of which go in part to the school. But how roundabout the path a nonchurch-school member must pursue in order to help children! The mere fact of being a member of a Christian Church ought to lay this duty upon him unmistakably, but it does not.

This is why it is so important to revamp our organization until it says in a language no one can misunderstand that the church itself is responsible for the Christian education of its children. In our present state of development perhaps the most feasible way of doing this is through a Board of Christian Education, elected by the whole congregation at the beginning of the year, caring for children in its name throughout the year, and submitting its report to the whole congregation at the year's close. Another decisive step in the right direction is to give up a separate church-school treasury, turn all school offerings into the church treasury, and then, reversing the process, include Christian education in the budget of the church itself. This is more than a fancy new style of bookkeeping. It is more than a device to get more money, although it may have that result. It is first and foremost a way of giving practical expression to an important conviction.

. . . .

The closing word of this discussion may well be by way of a warning. Unless a congregation is warmheartedly interested in its children, it cannot possibly educate them in the Christian religion no matter how technically perfect the program it sets up for them. It can construct a building of the latest design, replete with chapels, classrooms, blackboards, and what-not. It can secure the latest product of the lesson-writer's art. It can provide them with teachers who are masters of the Bible, adepts at teaching, and even lovers of the children; but unless the congregation itself loves the children all this is but sounding brass and clanging cymbal. They will know that they are being farmed out to a few experts who will conduct a program in their behalf, just as the children of a wealthy family with a quick flash of intuition sense what it means when they are given a governess and a nurse and an elaborate nursery. The children of a church may learn many things in such a situation, but they will not learn much about the Christian religion!

A church can give the Christian religion to its children only if it gives itself as well.

V

PUTTING THE SCHOOL BACK INTO
CHURCH SCHOOL

OCCASIONALLY someone facetiously asks, "When is a school not a school?" The answer that is expected and ofttimes given is, When it is a church school. Strange—is it not?—that the first Sunday school was a real school! Its sessions were five hours long, and it had paid teachers. At one stage in its development the Sunday-school sessions reached the astounding length of eight hours, from six to ten in the morning and from two to six in the afternoon.[1] It was a veritable school, meeting on Sunday. But in the course of time many of the features of a true school were stripped from it. The paid teacher gave way to the volunteer. The sessions were whittled down and whittled down until finally they spanned a mere hour, or less. Thus in time, with all its virtues, it reached such a low educational estate as to be the perfect example of a school which is not a school!

By no means do we want it to become a coldly academic institution to which reluctant scholars will drag themselves against their will. But we do want it to do good, consistent work. We do want its scholars to know more at the end of five years than they did at the beginning! There are some observers today who leap too hurriedly to the conclusion that this can never be. They are altogether discouraged by the nonedu-

[1] Brown, Arlo A., *A History of Religious Education in Recent Times.* The Abingdon Press, 1923, pp. 46 and 49.

cational pattern which has settled down upon the church school. They point out that, as things now stand, neither teachers, pupils, nor parents expect anything to be really learned! They contrast the manner in which boys and girls approach the public school with the manner of their approach to the church school—easygoing, lighthearted, dressed up in Sunday clothes, expecting primarily a social good time. And so they counsel the abandonment of the church school. But there would seem to be little gain in that. The church school is a great institution with marvelous potentialities. As it stands at present it numbers about 21,000,000 scholars—almost as many as the public school enrolls—with a force of 2,000,000 teachers and officers.[2] If we abandon it now, we might find ourselves merely under the necessity of setting up a new organization with the same name to accomplish the same purpose. The better part of wisdom is to capitalize upon it, and make the most of it. Hard as this may be, the alternatives might be harder.

If this is to be done, however, the ministers of Protestantism will have to assume the lead in most cases—and more vigorously than at present. A recent study of theological education brought out the incidental fact that among almost seven hundred ministers questioned on this point, only 5 per cent of their time was given to the educational work of their churches—a trifle more than they devoted to janitorial services.[3] (Another study in a selected group of churches served by graduates of theological seminaries revealed almost one fifth of the minister's time being given to the

---

[2] Douglass, H. P., and Brunner, E. deS., *The Protestant Church as a Social Institution.* Harper & Brothers, 1935, p. 159.

[3] *Ibid.*, p. 175.

church school.)[4] Without minimizing for a moment the magnificent service rendered by laymen and lay-women, we still must realize that the minister is sorely needed in the church school if it is ever to regain the status of a true school. His time is needed. His plans are needed. His presence is needed at board meetings, committee meetings, workers' conference meetings. His participation is needed—as a teacher sometimes, as a leader in worship on occasion, as a supervisor often, even as a superintendent in some churches. For the minister is the official leader of the church. He is in most cases the only person in a congregation who can devote his full time to the work of the church. Consequently, in the long run what he stresses will be stressed by the church.

Many ministers find themselves in the position of knowing full well the deficiencies of their schools, and having a rather clear notion of what they would like someday to achieve through them, but being at a loss as to how to begin. Can we locate some strategic places at which to take hold? The suggestions that follow do not have the few advanced schools in mind. Rather, they are offered for the great rank and file. They might be called "Ten Commandments for an Average Church School."

CREATING A HOLY DISSATISFACTION

Sometimes the finest service a minister can render his church school is to lead it tactfully to a noble discontent with its present achievement. For many schools suffer from low ideal-pressure. They are con-

---

[4] Hartshorne, H., Stearns, H. R., and Uphaus, W. E., *Standards and Trends in Religious Education.* The Yale University Press, 1933, p. 44.

tent so long as enrollment, attendance, and enthusiasm hold up fairly well. If the minister can open up for his school new vistas of possible achievement—without giving offense on the one hand nor unduly discouraging his workers on the other—he is taking the first long step toward a better school.

A visit to a good church school will sometimes accomplish this result admirably, or even a visit to a public school where the business of education is raised to a fine art. Sometimes the measurement of the school with Standard B of the International Council of Religious Education serves well to lay bare present deficiencies. One of the best ways of bringing home to a church school what it is and what it is not accomplishing is to measure the religious knowledge of its scholars with some objective test. The results are often surprising—and challenging! For example, a seminary student a few years ago undertook to find out how much boys and girls of church-membership age know about the life and teachings of Jesus. He gave one of the tests prepared by Northwestern University to 400 boys and girls twelve to fifteen years of age whose homes are in a deeply religious section of eastern Pennsylvania. The great majority of the four hundred were affiliated with some Protestant denomination and were members of a church school. The results almost pass belief.

> 209 did not know where to turn in the Bible to find the story of Jesus' life.
> 102 did not know where he was born.
> 167 did not know what occupation he followed.
> 250 did not know that he taught his followers the Lord's Prayer.
> 269 did not know that he grew up to young manhood in Nazareth.

127 did not know that he preached the Sermon on the Mount.

204 did not know by whom he was betrayed.

133 did not know that he was crucified between two thieves.

206 did not know that it was in the parable of The Good Samaritan that he taught how to be a good neighbor, rather than in the parables of The Ten Virgins, The Lost Sheep, or The Tares.

175 did not know what his first and great commandment was.

There was a difference of only 10 per cent between the general averages of those who went to church school and those who did not.

A few hours and a few dollars spent in such an inquiry in the average congregation might bring results that are wholly beneficent. They might induce the poverty of spirit which is the first stage in all true growth.

Intriguing People Into Studying

If true study is desired, there are only two ways to secure it. The one is to require it; the other is to lure people into it by intriguing their interest. When one comes to think of it, it is amazing how little we have done in the average church school along the line of this second and more excellent way. By way of contrast, there comes to mind the way in which a group of public-school children were led to study the life and culture of the Eskimos. They surrounded themselves in the schoolroom with pictures of Eskimo life. They made sleds, and igloos, and implements of reindeer bone (or what served for the time being to their fertile imaginations as reindeer bone). They read stories of Eskimos and their ways. The grand climax came one cold winter day when the children dressed to the full in coats, hats, and gloves, and threw the windows wide open. At that moment they ceased to be American children; they were Eskimos. They had entered dramatically into the life of another people. Consider now how tamely we undertake to teach the life and times of the Hebrew people—a few shabby quarterlies, the droning voice of a teacher who has herself probably not caught the glory of Hebrew life, and that is all. Is it any wonder that children don't study? The wonder is that they come at all.

There are so many things that can be done at little expense. They do cost, to be sure, some time and effort, but they are abundantly worth it. If a group of boys and girls are to study their community in the light of the Christian ideal, let them not remain behind closed doors but, rather, venture forth into that community to find out something about it. Let them make a housing survey (as a group of Intermediate boys did to their own satisfaction, if no one else's). Let them interview doctor, and judge, and mayor, and social worker. They will come back to study quarterlies and books, and gladly! If young people are to study the Negro in American life, let them visit Negroes, and be visited in turn. Paper and print were never intended to be a substitute for flesh and bone, but, rather, a supplement to them. If people, young or old, are to study war and peace, let them begin by preparing a drama which will sear their souls with the gravity of the issue—or at least let them read it. Then they will pore over facts and figures and pronouncements and Bible passages, and enjoy it. If boys and girls are to study the life of Jesus, let them assemble pictures of Jesus and the land where He lived, and construct in miniature the town of Nazareth, and trace with their own fingers on a map which they themselves have made the roads which He traversed. Such a study they will never forget.

And meanwhile let there be accumulating in the church-school quarters a veritable welter of maps, pictures, books, posters, curios, models, and magazines without number. They will accumulate if given a chance, and they are all hearty invitations to study. There can be maps for the wall and maps for the hand which will make Palestine as real as the next county. There can be a picture library, filed in a homemade filing cabinet and arranged by Biblical characters and books as well as by such contemporary topics as Nature, Home, School, Church, and the like. There can be a reference library of books for the pupil's own reading—interesting and attractive books which they will read without urging. There can be posters prepared by groups of young people to give striking presentation to some moral issue, or a graphic portrayal of some statistics on the frightful cost of war. There can be curios from the Holy Land, and from mission fields, and relics of the early history of the congregation. There can be models of the Temple at Jerusalem, and the first house of worship of the congregation in question, and a Moslem mosque, and whatever else the ingenuity and skill of the members can contrive. And even magazines can be made to serve the cause of Christian education! A file of selected copies of *The National Geographic* will help mightily when the lesson gets around to Arabia, or Egypt, or modern China.

Much that is here suggested can be achieved "without money and without price." It requires foresight and planning, and it requires the services of a custodian, and little more! The underlying strategy in this campaign to intrigue people into studying is twofold: first, to take the church school not infrequently out into the world; and, secondly, to bring the world vividly into the church school.

Fewer and Better Teachers

For a variety of reasons we have chopped many of our church schools into tiny classes. In many places a number of classes must meet in one room, and we have more or less instinctively kept the classes small in order that each little group might huddle about its teacher so as to hear above the noise of the other classes and in turn add as little to the noise as possible. Then, too, we have felt that a teacher would be able to know intimately all her pupils, if the class were small, and thus be in a position to bring spiritual help to them as individuals. At all events, while the public school has been going along with classes of twenty, thirty, or forty, we of the church school have had ten, eight, or six in a class. What has been the result? It seems we must now confess that it has fallen far short of our hopes! We have not succeeded in reducing the confusion materially. It is questionable whether ten classes of six each in one room are any quieter than four classes of fifteen. We have not succeeded, as we had hoped, in securing the personal touch in teaching. A distressingly large number of teachers are not sufficiently interested in their pupils to visit them in their homes or deal with them individually, even if there are only three or four of them. And—above all—we have been driven by this plan into a desperate effort to get enough teachers, in the course of which we have accepted not a few of inferior grade.

Might we not, then, clear the air tremendously and

open the way for better work by a change of policy to larger classes, and fewer and better teachers? There are, of course, limits beyond which this cannot be done, especially in small schools, for it is not possible to put a four-year-old and an eleven-year-old together merely for the sake of larger classes and fewer teachers. Furthermore, to inaugurate such a policy suddenly might give unwarranted offense. But, if a class is without a teacher, or a class's teacher has proved faithless, a judicious combination of classes can be made and the policy thus put into effect by easy stages. And there are other ways! In one department which formerly numbered twenty-four separate classes, a change was made to eight larger classes by the simple device of choosing the eight best qualified persons as head-teachers, and making the rest assistants. Consider how the problem of better work was immeasurably simplified by that one move. For one thing, a much higher quality of teaching was effected at once. It is doubtful if any other move could have possibly made as much difference in so short a time. Furthermore, the pastor, or the superintendent, could now work with that department as he could not possibly have done formerly. He could get his hands on the matter! There were now eight teachers to be dealt with, instead of twenty-four. Furthermore, curtains could now be hung—and were—to give each class a measure of privacy. That too was out of the question under the former regime. In short, while this change did not solve all the problems of that department, it did make them soluble.

One more consideration favoring this policy deserves to be mentioned here. With larger classes and fewer teachers it is within the range of possibility to pay each teacher a nominal sum per Sunday. It may be that some day we shall have to come to this, if we really desire to make the church school once more a school. All in all, it seems that one promising way out of our difficulties is fewer and better teachers.

TRAINING TEACHERS INTENSIVELY IN A FEW FUNDAMENTALS

Just as it is advantageous to reduce the number of teachers to a manageable size, so it is desirable also to fix our attention on a few items in their education which can be truly called fundamentals. Once this is done, the minister can keep pounding away eternally at these few fundamentals until they are well on the way to being mastered. It seems that these fundamentals are four in number.

Church-school teachers, generally speaking, need training in *the essentials of the Christian religion.* A group of teachers were once discussing how to make God real to their children. They soon volunteered the opinion that they were severely handicapped by His unrealness to them, the teachers. They had never thought through who God is, and what, and where, and how He deals with mankind. Many teachers would probably confess to a like vagueness with regard to Jesus and His significance, prayer, the content and value of the Bible, the sacraments, the Church, the Christian way of life, the Christian goal for society, and many other items of Christian belief. They need first of all not a better understanding of teaching method but a better understanding of the Christian religion. This is the first ringing challenge which comes to a minister from his teachers.

Church-school teachers need also to be *sensitized*

thoroughly to the individual needs of their pupils.
Lacking training in psychology, and overly impressed
with the need of teaching the Bible or some other
printed material, they all too often greet their pupils
warmly Sunday by Sunday, but they do not truly see
them. They do not see them as individuals, each one
standing in need of some unique revelation of Christian truth or some manifestation of human friendship
nicely suited to fit his own case. And, when they do
know them individually, they sometimes miss completely their chief needs. They are wide awake to the
harm of stealing and profanity, but miss completely
the perils which lurk in undue shyness. Therefore,
they need greatly to be sensitized, like a camera film,
to their pupils as individuals. Helpful and simply
written books on child and adolescent psychology,
like those of Dr. Douglas A. Thom,[5] may be eye-
openers to them. A group of teachers might well
undertake, under the pastor's guidance, to write
thumb-nail sketches of their individual pupils in accordance with an outline previously agreed upon. It
goes without saying that these sketches should be regarded as highly confidential. They are not for pub-
lication, but rather to train the teachers in clear-
sighted observation of the pupils for whose sake all
their teaching exists.

Yet another fundamental in which teachers need
intensive training is *the planning of a lesson.* Indeed,
this is the point at which most of them would desire
a pastor to begin. This is their work week in and week
out. Assistance given them here will make a maxi-

---

[5] *Everyday Problems of the Everyday Child.* D. Appleton-Century
Co., 1929. *Guiding the Adolescent.* Government Printing Office,
Washington, D. C., 1933.

mum change in their teaching immediately. For this reason it may be well to provide the teachers with a usable form for lesson-planning and encourage them to use it consistently for a month or so. Such unremitting discipline in lesson-planning, plus friendly discussion of some actual plans and the way they worked when put to the test, might remake the teaching of a school. The following plan is suggested for such a purpose. (It has a distinguished pedigree, including the outline given by Frances Cole McLester in her book, *What Is Teaching?*) The plan has been so drafted as to be applicable to classes of almost every age.

LESSON PLAN

1. *What is my exact aim in this lesson?* As a result of this lesson I want my scholars to be changed in the following ways: (E.g., to *know* the facts of Paul's life, or to *feel* grateful to parents, or to *do* their work well.)
2. *What will interest my class most in this connection?* Of all we might talk about or do in this lesson, what will appeal to them most? If left to themselves, what would they select as most interesting?
3. *What materials will I need?* (Bibles, newspaper clippings, poems, pictures, maps, pencils, etc.)
4. *How shall I start?* A good start gets their interest and prepares them for what is to follow. (Some ways of starting are: reviewing what we talked about last Sunday, showing a picture, telling a story or experience, free play, asking thought-provoking questions, etc.)
5. *What shall I do next, step by step?* (E.g., tell a story containing such and such a lesson, then get them to discussing the matter bringing out such and such points, then study certain verses in the Bible, etc.) Sometimes one can take the steps as given in the quarterly; often one must rearrange or add.

1.

2.

3.

4.

5.

6. *How shall I conclude?* A good conclusion summarizes, or drives the truth home. (E.g., the use of an appropriate picture, or a fitting poem, or a brief prayer, or asking the class to list their own conclusions.)

7. *What shall I do looking toward the next lesson?* Much of the success of a lesson depends on the last five minutes of the Sunday before. (E.g., turning to the next lesson and suggesting things to do in it, asking questions to whet interest, asking them to bring in newspaper clippings, deciding what questions to take up next Sunday, etc.)

This form can easily be fitted to a single typewritten page. It could be mimeographed in quantity, and used long enough to establish some mental habits which would stand the teachers in good stead as long as they remained in service.

Lastly, teachers need intensive training in *the use of a quarterly or text*. This is for many of them the chief resource in teaching, and it is highly important that they use it wisely. At present, it is often used unwisely. It is used slavishly, as though it were something sacrosanct rather than a mere set of suggestions for a happy, profitable experience for both teacher and class. Some teachers would regard it almost as sacrilege to omit a lesson, or expand one lesson to two Sundays, or rearrange the order of the lessons, or make an approach entirely different from that given in the quarterly. It is also frequently used piecemeal, as though each lesson were a separate unit. If we can help our teachers to see their quarterly or text "steadily and see it whole" and then use it with a wide freedom, we shall be rendering our schools a great service. For this purpose the most opportune time to act is several weeks before the beginning of each new quarter or unit of study. If several teachers are using the same course, they may well gather together for a solid evening of planning under competent guidance. What lies ahead during the coming quarter? What units of work constitute the quarter? Are there any lessons which will mean nothing to the classes in question? Is there any particular turn which the materials should be given in order to meet our classes' needs? What approaches are suggested by the lesson writer? Are they workable? What interesting things could be done in connection with the quarter's work? Are there any pictures or books or other materials which should be ordered now? Are there any special days during the quarter to be planned for and woven into the quarter's work, or any events in church or community that could be similarly dealt with? And so the questions run! The greatest worth of such a meeting is not for the months immediately ahead, but in the habits of work and thought which it will engender in the teachers of the school.

Using Visual Aids

So far as methods are concerned, it is reasonable to believe that the church school of the near future will make more and more use of the projector. If it does not, it will be missing an opportunity such as comes only once in a generation—or once in a century. The

commercial motion-picture interests have been kind
enough to stage a large-scale demonstration of the
efficacy of visual education. All that remains now is
for us to adapt their methods to our purposes. They
have shown us conclusively how the silver screen can
make real a great classic—exceeding by far the printed
page or the spoken word in vividness. In the short
space of two hours they have unrolled before our eyes
the intricate story of *David Copperfield* in such a
manner that we shall never forget it. To accomplish
the same result through the tedious medium of the
printed page requires hours upon end of hard reading.
If this can be done for *David Copperfield,* why not for
the Bible? They have shown us conclusively how the
motion picture can bring to life a character, such as
Uriah Heep. Anyone who has both seen and read
David Copperfield can readily test whether it is the
picturization or the verbal description of that famous,
falsely meek character which comes to mind when his
name is mentioned. But if this can be done for Uriah
Heep, why not for Saint Paul? Or David Livingstone?
Again, they have proved to us beyond a doubt and to
our great regret how potent the motion picture can be
in determining the actual conduct of the spectators.
The Payne Fund studies have revealed with scientific
exactness the extent to which the "movies" have contributed to juvenile delinquency. If this can be done
for low living, why not for high?

Every year—almost every month—brings some new
development in projecting apparatus or some new type
of film for the use of the church school. At this present
writing, films are available in the following areas: the
Holy Land; the life of Christ; the lives of Martin Luther and other leaders of the Church; the customs and

modes of living of the various peoples of the world; the many faiths of mankind; the parables of Jesus; the programs and activities of the several denominations; approved methods of church work; good Christian education procedure; and desirable ways of living in the ordinary social relationships.

What an array this is! And what an opportunity it opens to the church school which is in earnest about using its limited time to the best possible advantage! To be sure, the necessary equipment is as yet rather expensive, but the cost is not prohibitive—especially when we consider the speed of such education. If the showing of a film on the life of Christ costs ten dollars, and if as much is accomplished thereby in an hour or so as in six months of ordinary church-school teaching, can this really be accounted expensive?

It seems then that we ought to hold ourselves in readiness to take full advantage of this promising new method. The bulletin entitled *Visual Aids in the Service of the Church,* published by the Harmon Foundation for the Yale Divinity School, contains a stimulating account of recent developments in this field.

More Time for Class Sessions

The public school would not attempt for a moment to teach in the amount of time which the average church school has at its disposal. Imagine the reaction of a public-school teacher if the superintendent or the patrons should say to her: "We should like you to teach our children arithmetic. You may have them once a week for a period of twenty or twenty-five minutes. Not to mention the fact that they will not come regularly, and that you will have to meet in the same room with four other classes, and that we can give you little equipment to speak of, we feel we ought to tell you that there will be quite a few special days throughout the year when we shall have to forego the lesson period altogether. We wish you much success in your venture." It is not difficult to forecast the teacher's answers. As a matter of fact, the average church-school teacher has about as much time with her class in a whole year as a public-school teacher has in one week.

There are not a few church schools which have solved this problem by expanding the session to considerably more than an hour. This is a worthy solution, and one toward which we ought to work wherever possible. However, for the rank and file of schools, this way out is not an easy one. It demands a high caliber of teaching, a willingness on the part of teachers to miss the morning church service, and rooms from which no sound of children's voices carries over into the church sanctuary to disturb the morning devotions.

There are other solutions to this problem of inadequate time—notably the weekday school and the vacation school. Both of these deserve abundantly to be used wherever possible. But it still remains true that for the majority of church schools the quickest and simplest solution lies in the direction of a better use of the one hour which they now have. More specifically, the one easiest way to secure more time for teaching in the average school is to take less time for worship—particularly with adolescents and adults. The children under twelve present a different situation altogether. But for those of sufficient age to worship with the congregation in the church service there seems no good reason for taking half of a precious church-school hour for worship. Often it is not worship at any rate; and when it is, its very excellence may stand in the way of attendance at the church service.

Let the church-school worship, then, for the ages mentioned, be reduced to a mere ten minutes. Immediately there is available a clear forty-five minutes for the class session. Furthermore, a part of this can be devoted to guided study, for which there is great need. It seems a forlorn hope to expect that many church-school members in our generation will take lesson materials home to study them there. The only reasonable alternative, then, is to provide a time for such study within the school hour itself. We visualize, therefore, a teacher settling down with her class to a substantial forty-five-minute period. Quarterlies, Bibles, and the like are produced. Teacher and class together remind themselves of the specific purpose of this session. They fix their minds definitely on a few things to look for in their materials. The teacher says, "I think you will find the story on page twenty-four of especial interest," or "There is a point on page twenty-six which bears particularly on today's discussion." And then, with the teacher following them in spirit and stimulating them and guiding them at intervals, the class members settle down to some honest study. Twenty minutes may be spent thus. This is little enough, but it is a thousand times better than nothing at all. Imperceptibly, perhaps, the transition is then made to a discussion of the problem for the day in the light of the reading which has been done. And thus— through the single device of more available time—another sizable step is taken toward good workmanship.

MORE REGULAR ATTENDANCE

One of the prime obstacles to educational and spiritual efficiency in the church school is the scattered, irregular attendance with which we are plagued in every part of the country. The percentage of attendance in the public school is on the upper side of 90 per cent. Any minister can discover what percentage obtains in his own church school. The chances are good that it will hover around 60 per cent. Now, the simple truth of the matter is that it is unthinkable to expect really good work with such a percentage of attendance, even though the teachers be educational experts and spiritual saints and the equipment all that the heart can desire. We can drop stray bits of inspiration into the hearts of the casual attendants, and we can perhaps keep them identified with the church and with church people, but we cannot teach the life of Christ, nor the history of the Church, nor the origin and content of the Bible, nor the Christian doctrine of God, nor the Christian view of international relationships. There is no point in deceiving ourselves— it cannot be done! And it needs greatly to be done, if we are to avoid religious illiteracy.

How shall we secure more regular attendance? Through prizes and awards? Hardly! These work for the few, but not for the many; and even with the few there are questionable by-products. It goes without saying that our first reliance must be lodged in making the program itself so interesting and meaningful that the members of the school will refuse to miss it. Beyond this, it is possible to accomplish much by educating pupils and parents in season and out of season concerning the necessity of regular attendance. A letter to the parents of a class which is about to take up an important study, telling them of the study and asking their co-operation during the months ahead;

an *occasional* reporting of how many pupils have attended ten or eleven times during the past quarter (perfect attendance is not so important, nor is the total number present on a given Sunday); a consideration of this problem of attendance by the official board, and even by the whole congregation at its annual meeting—these may help. They may serve to provide the moral equivalent of the truant officer. Yet a further step of value is to institute a truly careful follow-up of absentees. It matters not what system is adopted for doing this, just so long as it is done, for a series of two or three unexplained absences is a serious matter, as is a spotty attendance record for an individual over a period of months. Both mean that the school is partially failing with the pupil in question, and that he may conceivably be lost to the church entirely. Therefore, both richly merit the careful attention of no less a person than the pastor. A visit today may mean a member kept tomorrow.

A THREE-MONTHS' SPECIAL STUDY-PROJECT

In our search for levers to raise the level of church-school work, we dare not pass by the possibilities which reside in a special study-project engaging an entire congregation with all its auxiliaries for a period of several months. The plan has so many uses, and so many values, that it may be well to note how it actually worked out in a given church. This congregation seized upon the four hundredth anniversary of the printing of the first English Bible as an occasion for centering its entire life for a season in the Book of books. The attractive prospectus of this undertaking, with some omissions and deletions of names, ran as follows:

116

PUTTING SCHOOL BACK INTO CHURCH SCHOOL

A THREE-MONTH CONGREGATION-WIDE EMPHASIS ON THE BIBLE—HOW WE GOT IT, WHAT IS IN IT, HOW TO USE IT, WILL MARK OUR FALL PROGRAM FOR 1935

The Church School

The curriculum in all departments will be Bible-centered, and will include courses in such fields as "The General Content of the Bible," "How We Got Our Bible," "How to Use the Bible," "Heroes and Heroines of the Bible," and "Studying the Bible with Crayon and Paintbrush."

The Woman's Missionary Society

At the September meeting the W. M. S. will sponsor a public presentation of "The Book Goes Forth," consisting of picture slides with explanatory lecture showing how the Bible is distributed in foreign lands. At the October meeting the theme will be "Missionaries as Bible Translators."

The Men's League

A symposium on "What the Bible Means to Me" will feature the meeting on September 18; and for the meeting on October 16 it is hoped to have a capable speaker give an address on "Miles Coverdale and the English Bible."

The Young People's Sunday Evening Meetings

A short Bible dramatization is planned for Sunday evening, September 29, and several others will likely be given later. A discussion on "Does It Matter What the Bible Says?" will be followed by a series of discussions on "What the Bible says about: Gambling, Liquor, War, Religious Persecutions, Sunday Movies, etc."

The Morning Worship Service

The fall program will be inaugurated at the morning worship service on September 15 with a sermon on "The Bible: Book of Books." The following Sunday a Family

Service of Worship will be held, and the minister will preach on "The Family Bible." A series of sermons will follow on "Bible Discoveries of God": "Abraham—God Is Universal"; "Moses—God Is Sovereign"; "Amos—God Is Justice"; "Hosea—God Is Mercy"; "Jesus—God Is Love"; and "Paul—God Is All-Inclusive."

A Congregational Pageant

An elaborate pageant, "Let There Be Light!" by Elliot Field, will be given on Thursday evening, November 21. This pageant-drama will depict the long story of the development of the Bible and of its influence on civilization.

The Book and Exhibit Room

The Junior Department assembly room on the first floor will be used as a Bible exhibit room. In addition to suggestive wall-posters, there will be a display of large cards showing pages from many foreign-language Bibles. There will be pamphlets for free distribution, and a variety of good Bibles and helps for the study of the Bible which may be ordered through the person in charge of the table.

Twelve Weekly Lectures

The members of the faculties of our college and seminary—men who are recognized masters in their respective fields of Bible study—will offer a series of lectures on successive Tuesday evenings. Some of the themes will be: "The Old Testament"; "The New Testament"; "The Bible and Other Sacred Books"; "Why the Bible Was Translated Into the Common Languages"; "The Bible and Social Justice"; and "What Makes the Bible the Word of God."

The merits of such a congregation-wide study-project are many and obvious. Not least among these is its probable effect upon a church school that for many years has known little besides a routine following of quarterlies. For here the spell of the quarterly is broken. For three glorious months the classes undertake a study because they want to—not because a quarterly says so. The congregational study-project, therefore, may be set down as an excellent device for breaking the grip of tradition and setting a people free.

"Electives" for Young People and Adults

It is difficult to exaggerate the new lease on life which a church school might experience from placing the curriculum of its young people's and adult classes on an elective basis. The chief benefit of such a step is not at all by way of securing better study materials than the quarterlies now in use, although that may well happen. The chief benefit is rather in the minds of the scholars. They have for so long taken the school, its quarterlies, and its indifferent teaching for granted. The beginning of a new quarter rolls around; the members of the classes look rather halfheartedly to see what is to be taken up during the coming months (after all, it doesn't matter greatly what it is); the quarterly announces such and such a topic; and that is that! Suppose, now, the question of what is to be studied is hurled back into their own laps. There is now nothing that they *have* to study as a matter of course. Perhaps now for the first time in their lives they will begin to consider what they *want* to study, and what they *need* to study. This single experience may radically transform their attitude toward the school, and galvanize them into interested, active participation.

This, however, is far from a simple step. It is beset on all sides by difficulties and dangers. First of all is the financial difficulty. The subject of study selected by a class may require books costing three to six times

119

what the usual quarterly would cost. This, however, may prove to be the easiest difficulty to circumvent. If the school will purchase the required materials, put its own imprint upon them, issue them for the period of the study, and then reclaim them for use again and again, it will in the long run spend no more than it would for quarterlies and have much more to show for what it does spend. But there is the further difficulty of knowing where to secure proper materials for the areas of study chosen by the several classes. This class desires to study war and peace from the Christian standpoint, and that class of an entirely different age is anxious for a study of the life of Christ. What suitable materials are there, and where can they be procured? Strangely enough, the adult classes seem more nearly ready for such a move than the young people's. Educational Bulletin No. 410 of the International Council of Religious Education, entitled *Learning for Life,* contains an admirable listing of study materials for all the areas that the average class is likely to enter. It is almost equally valuable for the older young people's classes. For the young people, the booklets of the "Christian Youth Building a New World" program are themselves usable study guides, and besides, list the titles of many others classified according to the ten areas into which this program is divided. To supplement these a postcard to three or four leading denominational publishing houses will bring catalogues of young people's and adult elective courses which almost bury the inquirer under the wealth of available material.

Another major difficulty is that of securing and training teachers properly qualified to handle an elective curriculum. Such a plan is a far cry from the

International Uniform Lessons, and demands much more of the teachers. It should not be tried, until the teachers are ready. A Senior High School Department of a church school in a college community waited and planned five years for this step, before its exceptionally capable leader felt the teaching staff was fully prepared. To go into the elective system prematurely would spell not good education, but chaos.

There is a danger involved in this step—and a real one. It is that the several classes may suffer from a poorly balanced spiritual diet. In a school where this procedure had been in use for some years the officers suddenly awoke one day to the realization that some classes had not in five or ten years given any real consideration to the life of Jesus. It is, therefore, essential that someone in the school—or, better still, a number working together—draw up a statement of the more important areas of study which the classes of the several ages ought to get around to sooner or later. This becomes a check-list with which the actual record of each class's curriculum year by year may be compared.

Promotion Day—A Point of Leverage

There remains to be considered an unassuming special day in the school's calendar—namely, Promotion Day. It is quite commonly observed on the last Sunday of September. On this day pupils are promoted with appropriate ceremony and ritual from one department to another, and sometimes from one class to another.

To all of us who are deeply concerned over raising the standards of church-school work, there comes the haunting suggestion that perhaps in Promotion Day we may find a point of leverage for accomplishing this result. What would happen if we were to transform it by easy stages into a genuine Commencement Day, to be held either in spring or fall as seemed best? There is a limit, of course, beyond which we dare not go. We are scarcely in a position to "flunk" anyone in church school, but we might at least give open recognition to good work done and thus begin to impress the conviction that church school is a place where good work can be done. It is not overly difficult to imagine a statement such as the following being made by superintendent or pastor as he calls a class of adolescents before him for promotion: "This class has, among other things, studied the life of Christ during the past six months. It has demonstrated its knowledge of the subject in the charts which you will find in the adjoining room for your examination and in the well-informed and reverent essay to which you have just listened. The class was of service to three needy families during the past winter. It also made a special study of the issues involved in the last election, viewing them always from the Christian standpoint. In short, this class has given clear proof of its ability to carry on the Christian enterprise on a new level. Worthy of special mention is the work of one member of the class, who doubtless prefers to remain nameless. He has written his own Life of Christ in no little detail, and has shown himself particularly skillful in the difficult art of dealing helpfully with unfortunate people." Such a statement could be dignified, reserved, and without the slightest tinge of unchristian flattery.

This is for most schools only a dream as yet, but it is not an impossible dream. Promotion Day may yet become a high point of the year toward which a church school works, and from which it works.

VI

TRAINING FOR CHURCH MEMBERSHIP

ONE of the long-standing criticisms of the religious education movement has been that it failed to give proper attention and honor to the Christian Church. Its leaders themselves have not been greatly interested in the Church (so the indictment runs), and they have shown no consuming zeal to make the Church central in the lives of the children and young people whom they have taught. The temptation is great to rush to the defense of the movement. It might be said, for example, with considerable truth that the Church had been overemphasized and needed badly a deflation of its institutional ego. Another line of defense would be to pile up the evidence that within the last decade or so the Christian education movement has actually made a great deal of the Church. There is an abundance of such evidence. For some years now one of the seven avowed objectives of the International Council of Religious Education, comprising more than forty of the leading Protestant denominations, has been to relate people helpfully, intelligently, loyally to the Christian Church. Nor has this objective received mere lip-service. It has found its way into lesson courses, hymns, and other worship materials, and the books written by Christian educators. Indeed, the International Council of Religious Education recently selected as its central emphasis for an entire year "Christ in the Life of the Church." All of this, and more, is true. Yet, when all this has been said, the original indictment still contains a measure of truth which ought not be passed over too lightly.

It is easy to see why Christian education should have fallen into the error of minimizing the Church. To begin the story a century and a half ago, the Sunday school was not founded in a church, nor by official action of any church body, nor by a professional leader of the church. It was started in a private dwelling by a printer who acted solely on his own initiative. It would have been splendid if the Church had sponsored it officially while it was still wrapped in swaddling clothes, but this was not the case. In time the Sunday school did receive a tardy baptism into the ecclesiastical fold, but the baptism was only partially successful. Nothing shows this more clearly than the fact that its leaders have typically been outstanding laymen, rather than ministers. It has on occasion even been forced to hold its sessions in a public-school building because the Church would not give it a home.

Then, around the turn of the century, the religious education movement burst into full flower. Again in this new stage the leaders of the movement were not identified primarily with the Church—either in their own minds, or in the minds of others. They were scientists, psychologists, educators. They ofttimes felt called upon to sit in judgment upon the Church, and the Church was not slow to return the favor. Besides, their primary interest was not in any institution, but in people—first, last, and always. It was almost inevitable, therefore, that a breach should open up between the Church on the one hand and Christian education on the other. This breach, unfortunately, was widened further by the policy which was adopted for developing professional leaders for the new movement. This policy took the form not so much of educating ministers in the insights and skills of Christian education, but, rather, of setting up separate schools for the training of a separate set of leaders who would be called Directors of Religious Education. How different the situation today might be if the Christian education movement had from the beginning concentrated its efforts on the theological seminaries! The Church might feel a little kindlier toward Christian education, and Christian education might be more aware of the Church.

So much for the past! It is a story which we would change at certain points if we could, but of course we cannot. All we can now do is to look to the present and future. The present scene seems to indicate that Christian education—without sacrificing for a moment its primary concern for people—needs to pay real attention to the Church.

THE NEED FOR PROTESTANT CHURCHMANSHIP

The sad truth is that churchmanship—a sense of the importance of the Church and loyalty to it—threatens to reach a low-water mark in American Protestantism. In order to put this to the test it is necessary only to announce the hymn "I Love Thy Kingdom, Lord." The familiar lines—"I love thy Church, O God! . . . For her my tears shall fall. . . . Beyond my highest joy I prize her heavenly ways"—fall rather strangely upon many modern ears. In so far as this is true of us, it is natural that we should find ourselves failing ofttimes to develop a new generation loyal to the Church.

If our churchmanship at present threatens to be feeble and anemic, why should this be so? We can readily find one answer, at least, in the fact that the old denominational loyalties are going with nothing to take their place. These old loyalties were abominable, but they did have one merit—they did attach people strongly to the Church. It may be that we have vigorously swept clean the rooms of the soul, but have been at no pains to refurnish them in an ampler style.

However, this is merely a superficial answer. The true fault lies considerably deeper—within the very nature of Protestantism. Protestantism has never had a very strong sense of the Church. The early Reformers had had enough Church, and to spare. The weight of the institution had borne down upon them until their souls were almost crushed, so they threw it off manfully and much that went with it. Standing erect, then, in their new freedom, the Reformers went on to fashion the characteristically Protestant doctrine of "the universal priesthood of believers." The intent of this was unmistakable. By it they meant to say that the individual could now speak to God and God to the individual "without benefit of clergy" and—what is more, to our present point—without the intercession of the Church. At least the Church did not hold the same monopoly on the roads between man and God as formerly. The priest was gone, and—in a real sense— the Church was gone. In a limited yet true sense the earthly unit with which the Almighty had dealings was no longer an institution, or a body of believers even, but the individual. This is "rugged individualism" with a vengeance, and it was part and parcel of the Protestant Reformation. Add to all of this the political doctrines which broke upon the world in full force at the time of the French and American Revolutions, and there is no longer any need to wonder why we have two hundred Protestant denominations! The wonder is that we do not have more!

We are eternally grateful for this release of the individual both in politics, commerce, and religion. However, we are now beginning to see rather dimly in all of these realms that there is something lacking in the mere notion of millions of independent individuals—each one a law unto himself. It is beginning to dawn upon us that we cannot run government that way, nor business, nor religion. That way is beginning to look considerably like a blind alley, blocked at the end by a new Tower of Babel!

It may well be that, without yielding up one iota of "the freedom wherewith Christ has made us free," we now need to recover more of the notion that the unit with which God deals is often a group rather than a solitary individual. His ultimate objective, of course, is the individual heart, but perchance He can best arrive there on occasion by way of a group. There is nothing unfamiliar about this idea. It does not jar at all upon our Protestant sensibilities to think of God as reaching an individual through the family group. Why should it offend us to think of Him as reaching an individual through the church group? In this connection it is rather significant that the Buchmanite movement has recently come to be known quite generally as the "Groups" movement and its members as "Groupers." What does this language signify, if not the firm belief of this movement that a group, not an individual, is the true spiritual unit? One need not agree with all or even most of the Buchmanite tenets to appreciate the worth of this notion.

All of this bears directly upon the need for a stronger Protestant churchmanship. We do not want a recrudescence of the old bitter denominational loyalties. God forbid! No more do we want a hierarchical institution lording it over the souls of men! It is not an institutional emphasis at all which we need, so much as it is a group emphasis. What our centrifugal Protestantism now needs, it would seem, is a sense of the Church as an organism, made up of individuals who are the members of the organism and so important both to those individuals and to the world at large that it deserves some clear attention in its own right. Modern sociology would call this organism "a primary social group," and would speak in extravagant terms of its high importance. Historic Christianity has long called it much more beautifully "the body of Christ"—not an organization, nor an institution, but a body of which Christ is the infusing spirit and of which all we are members. It is a marvelous thing— this body! It is a living, breathing organism—now nineteen hundred years old. And yet it is the same body, just as our physical bodies retain their identity year by year even though not a single cell which composed them years ago should remain today. And the spirit in it is the same through all generations. "*There is* one body, and one Spirit, even as also ye were called in one hope of your calling; one Lord, one faith, one baptism, one God and Father of all, who is over all, and through all, and in all."

To become a member of this body in deed and in truth is no light thing. It deserves to be thought of highly, to be prepared for carefully, and to be accomplished finally with a fitting and memorable ceremony.

THE CHURCH-MEMBERSHIP CLASS

By no means the only way, but just as certainly one worthy way, of moving toward a higher type of Protestant churchmanship is to make much of the church-membership class. Certain denominations—notably the Lutheran, Episcopalian, and Reformed groups—have observed this practice since the days of the Reformation. It is very significant that the practice appears to be spreading at the present time. A recent study of some seven hundred churches (not quite typical churches, for only those served by graduates of theological seminaries were included) revealed that 57 per cent of these ministers held confirmation classes regularly.[1] Certain it is that denominations which do not belong to any of the groups above mentioned are now issuing manuals for church-membership classes, and urging their use.

There are excellent reasons for the widespread adoption of the church-membership class. Even if the church schools were to do their work perfectly (which they do not) so that boys and girls came to church-membership age fully instructed concerning the Church, its doctrines, and its usages, the church-membership class would still be needed. It would still have the two invaluable functions of magnifying to its proper size the experience of joining the church, and of affording the pastor intimate contact with each successive band of young recruits to his church. This last is regarded by many pastors as one of the choicest privileges of the entire ministry. In fact, it is not unknown for a minister to group his congregation mentally into two classes—those who have joined the church under his tutelage, and those who have not. So much do these hours of personal contact with incoming members mean to him!

[1] Hartshorne, H., Stearns, H. R., and Uphaus, W. E., *Standards and Trends in Religious Education.* The Yale University Press, 1932, p. 49.

The details of administering the church-membership class vary widely, and necessarily so. The weekly meetings are commonly held throughout the late fall and winter months, leading up to confirmation (or its equivalent) on Palm Sunday. Country pastors, however, often find it more convenient to meet in the summer and adjacent seasons, at which times the roads are a little more kindly disposed toward church activities. A weekday hour is probably used most frequently, but not a few ministers are utilizing the regular church-school hour for this purpose. As to the length of the term during which the class is held, a growing tendency is to extend the instruction over a two-year period—partly because the work of the church school at present is so poor that the minister can take virtually nothing for granted. There is an added advantage in this two-year plan in that it provides a good excuse for raising by one year the age of joining the church. If the customary age has been twelve, there is real gain in advancing it to thirteen or even fourteen. By that time these early adolescents are considerably more mature, and in a much better position to comprehend to the full the significance of the step they are taking.

The really troublesome problem concerns the scope of the course. There are so many things that might be dealt with, and so little time in which to deal with them—even in a two-year class. *Perhaps the safest clue to follow here comes from a proper understanding of the true purpose of the class.* Is it primarily doctrinal —to give these young people a slightly diluted and popularized course in Systematic Theology? Or is it primarily ethical—to unfold the Christian way of life in all its implications for both personal and social living? *If it is neither of these, but, rather, to prepare adolescents for full, intelligent, loyal membership in the Christian Church, then the outline of the course begins to assume definite shape accordingly.* It would seem, in this case, that its chief "units" ought to be the following:

1. Informal conversation for discovering how the class members feel about the church—what it means to them, what they like about it and what they dislike, what they know and do not know about it, why they are planning to join the church, what this step signifies to them, and the like.
2. Consideration of the church's machinery—its officers, meetings, auxiliaries, its affiliation with other agencies, its denominational program, institutions, and judicatories. Also its finances—how much money is required, where it goes to, and their own responsibilities in this regard.
3. Interpretation of the church's services—its regular services (especially in a liturgical church), the communion service, the rites employed at the time of joining the church, etc.
4. Brief survey (if time permits and interest warrants) of the Church's history—local, denominational, and universal. Such a study, well done, may enhance greatly their sense of privilege in affiliating with so noble an institution. One of the best ways of doing this seems to be in terms of the lives of the great leaders of the Church from Jesus to our own day. (Tucker, *Builders of the Church*, The Abingdon Press, is an excellent guide for this.)
5. Above all, a thorough examination of the Church's present purpose and program—what it undertakes to do for individuals and for society, and the strategy it employs in both cases. (Versteeg, *Christianity at Work*, The Abingdon Press, contains much usable material for such a study.) In this connection boys and girls probably need a chance to think through carefully what Jesus meant and what we mean by

131

the kingdom of God for which the Church exists. How can they devote their lives to working for that which they do not understand?

6. As much attention to questions of doctrine—God, Jesus, sin, salvation, immortality, and the like—as is absolutely necessary to their assumption of full membership in the church. The amount of time devoted to this will depend in part upon the thoroughness with which the church school has done its work, and in part also on the questions they ask.

7. As much attention to questions of Christian ethics —living in the home, at school, use of leisure time, relations between the sexes, social issues—as is absolutely necessary to their full membership in the church. Again, the minister can be governed by their prior preparation and by the perplexities or misunderstandings they reveal in class discussion.

This is merely a tentative list of possible areas to be explored, and the order in which they are here given has no significance whatsoever. With the exception of the first, they might just as well have been arranged in any other order. The only proper order is the one that proves most natural for a given class, and that will probably vary greatly from year to year. Perhaps a minister's first reaction in surveying a list of this sort is one of despair in the face of the enormity of the task. And truly it is enormous. Here is work enough not for one winter or two, but for a lifetime? Unless some of these "units" should prove unnecessary, there seems to be only one good way out of the difficulty—namely, to work in season and out for the improvement of the church school, especially during the Intermediate years of twelve to fourteen. One workable plan is for the minister to take under his special pastoral oversight the Intermediate classes of the church school—examining their lesson courses to make sure they include what is needful, choosing their teachers with care, guiding them in their task, and, in short, regarding these classes as an integral part of his plan of preparation for church membership.

The choice of materials for the class's work will be governed, likewise, by the purpose to be achieved. If this purpose is thought of as being chiefly doctrinal, then something can be said for making a catechism the chief source of instruction. If, on the other hand, the chief intent is seen to be something other than doctrinal, the catechism becomes only one among several materials to be used. Another serious limitation upon the usefulness of catechisms in the church-membership class is the fact that none of them were written by adolescents, nor were they as a rule prepared by authors who understood adolescents. Consequently, they describe religion in terms ofttimes foreign to the experience of modern boys and girls, and in language which they cannot understand. Quite a few denominations are at the present time issuing valuable manuals for use in the church-membership class. Among the best nondenominational guides for the class discussions is Lobingier, *Our Church* (The University of Chicago Press).

The choice of methods too will be determined by the purpose sought. If our objective is nothing less than to fit young disciples for responsible membership in the Christian Church, mere lecturing to them will not do—no matter how inspiring it may be. We run the great risk in this method of missing half the points which trouble them most. Nor will mere memorization of the catechism, the Bible, or any other books! What seems to be called for principally is friendly, serious, purposeful conversation on important topics of the Church and the Kingdom, together with actual study of the church budget, an actual visit to an official-board meeting, and the like. Perhaps we ought to visualize the sessions of a church-membership class as following such a pattern in the main. However, even this is not enough. There ought to be, in addition, brief periods of real worship in the class sessions, in the leadership of which the boys and girls themselves might well have a part. Perhaps some of them have never experienced true worship until this moment. But even this is not sufficient. People do not become a true part of a fellowship merely by talking about it. They must also be given a chance to become one with it through doing something for it, and for the causes which it loves. This may consist merely of distributing the copies of the parish bulletin, but who shall call that trivial? Such an experience may be remembered by a boy or girl long after the hours of talking are forgotten.

In order to come to closer grips with the method of the church-membership class, it may be valuable to cite the plans employed by some pastors, with a few accompanying comments.

A useful practice is that of taking the class on pilgrimages, so to speak, to points of religious interest. The destination may be a denominational college, or orphanage, or a historic church edifice. Or—with a somewhat different purpose—it may be a congregation of another denomination, or a church with a rich and varied program, or the headquarters of some agency with and through which the church works. Such pilgrimages are nothing new in the public school. Neither are they in the Christian Church, for that matter!

Some ministers, in casting about for ways in which the class can have a part in the life of the church, recommend turning over to them the task of ushering at the Sunday services of worship—at least for a specified period. Another way of accomplishing the same end is to enlist them as canvassers in the Every Member Canvass. They cannot, of course, go out alone, but they can go in the company of older and more experienced members—two by two in keeping with ancient precedent.

Ministers generally make a special effort to inculcate in the members of the class the habit of regular attendance at the Sunday morning service of worship. One minister, for example, tells his class that they will meet twice a week—once, say, on Friday night, and again on Sunday morning at eleven o'clock. They are expected, then, to to be in their proper places at that hour, and their presence is often noted in a special collect in the morning prayer. Furthermore, they are asked at the next meeting of the class to report upon the sermon and the service of the Sunday before. There can be no doubt that it is important to stress church attendance at this stage in their lives, and doubly and triply important if we find ourselves taking the position that up to the age of full church membership children should not be expected to attend church regularly. Perhaps we can accomplish most toward this worthy end by taking the members of the class with us, as it were, on the inside of the morning church service. Their help can be solicited in the choice of the hymns. On occasion the sermon itself can be planned to deal with some vital issue which has come up in the class and which promises to be of interest to the congregation as a whole. If the members of the class can be brought to feel that the service is in a measure their service, they will be more likely to want to come, and come again.

One minister—there are probably many others—makes it a point to hold an individual conference with each member of his church-membership class. For this purpose he visits the home of the member, and the whole family—indeed, the whole congregation—know the reason for his coming. In this way he makes sure that the peculiar doubts and difficulties of each individual will have a chance to be dealt with, and also that each prospective church member will face squarely the full meaning of the step which he is about to take.

Of particular interest is the plan worked out by one minister for correlating the discussions in his church-membership class with the successive events in the life of his congregation. His strategy is to take up a matter in the class at the very time when that same matter is to the fore among his people. In this way he contrives to "strike while the iron is hot." There follow a few illustrations of the operation of this plan:

Nov. 13—The work of Home Missions. The congregation observed Home Mission Day.

Nov. 20—The income of the local church; the use of church envelopes; stewardship. The congregation observed "Volunteer Day" when pledges for the coming year were made. The class helped address the packets of church envelopes.

Dec. 25—The relief work of the church: ministerial relief and sustentation; homes for the aged and orphans. Pupils reported on visits to these homes. The offering from the evening service was sent to a denominational orphans' home.

Jan. 1—The elements of worship and their significance. The congregation used the service preparatory to the Holy Communion.

Feb. 12—The work of Foreign Missions. The congregation observed Foreign Mission Day.

This is only a partial list. It is surprising at how many points the class sessions can be made to parallel the life of the congregation. Of course this plan sacrifices logical order very largely, but it may more than make up for this loss by the vitality and timeliness which it gains.

It is a common practice in many churches to bring the period of instruction to a close with a more or less public examination, to which the members of the official board and the parents of the class members are especially invited. The problem here is to make the examination as vital as possible to the incoming members. One possible way of doing this is to devote the closing sessions of the class to a careful formulation of first the beliefs and secondly the purposes which these young people cherish as they stand at the threshold of church membership. At the "examination" time these statements might be read by members of the class, and followed with questions asked by the class as well as of them.

In ways such as these the minister may do his best to incorporate these new members within "the body of Christ." At last the day of their full induction into church membership arrives—and the real test begins. The "mortality rate" during this first year is often high —high enough to discourage thoroughly the faithful minister. Is there anything to be done about it? One possibility is to allow the church-membership class to continue for a while—less frequently perhaps and not so formally, but just enough to keep alive the contact between the minister and the new members. It goes without saying that every possible effort should be made to find ways in which the new members can take their part in the church fellowship—work that they can do, congenial organizations that they can join, and the like. Whatever we do in this regard will grow out of the realization that the year after joining the church is every whit as important to a young person's church relationship as the year before.

CHILDREN AND THE CHURCH SERVICES

Important as is the church-membership class, there can be no doubt that training children for church membership involves much more than a special course of a year or so. How simple the matter would be if that were all that was required! But as a matter of fact a child is trained for or against church membership by all the contacts he has with the church from babyhood on. Every time it touches his life it is molding his relation to it either for good or for ill.

Of special significance among these contacts is the child's experiences with the services of the church. We want the little child to love these services when he is grown to manhood. At the same time we have no right to sacrifice his present happiness and Christian growth to some future goal—no matter how worthy that goal may be. What, then, shall be our policy concerning children and the church services? Shall we expect them to attend the morning church worship regularly, or not? Which will be better for them? For the church? For the Kingdom? There is no more knotty problem in the whole field of Christian education than this one.

There are those who plead earnestly for a return to the practice of the *Family Pew*, with mother, father, and all the children sitting side by side every Sunday morning in their accustomed place. The advocates of the Family Pew feel strongly that much of religion's strength in by-gone days was due to the faithful observance of this practice, and that we cannot hope for a religious revival in our own day without it. The reasons for it run along familiar lines. This is the true way—so the proponents of the Family Pew maintain—to train children in regular church attendance. The essential thing in such training is to begin early, so that a child shall never know anything else than being in his regular place on the Lord's day.

"Train up a child in the way he should go,
And when he is old he will not depart from it."

Furthermore, the Family Pew is the real way to train children in worship. It makes no great difference whether they understand what is said and sung, or not. What matters is their presence in a place whose associations are sacred, and where they may see mother and father and neighbors and friends in the attitude of prayer. Besides these two weighty reasons there is the further consideration that the Family Pew is a strong tie for binding together the several members of a family. Those who have been thus bound to one another will be better able to resist the evil tendencies of modern life which threaten to break down home life and pull the family into little pieces.

Reasons such as these appeal not only to our minds but also to our hearts—and perhaps that very fact ought to be taken as a warning signal to stop and consider carefully! It is difficult for us to think clearly about this matter, because so many of us who are adults within the church today came up through just such a regime. Consequently, when we begin to reflect upon it, there come welling into our minds a host of memories which are very precious but which do not help us particularly to think accurately. For example, the Family Pew may have had the desired effect in our cases, but what of the others? There are today millions of people in America outside the Church. How many of them also came up through the experience of the Family Pew, but were turned against the Church rather than toward it? It is by no means uncommon to hear a person say: "Yes, I had to go to church as a child, but the moment I was able to make my own decisions I stopped going." That sort of reaction too must be admitted as evidence. Modern psychology teaches clearly that mere repetition is not enough to build an act or an experience into a habit; there must also be a deep, abiding satisfyingness in the act if it is ever to arrive at the status of a habit. But let us go a step further. Do we really want church attendance to be a habit? Do we want people to attend because they have been trained to it, as a dog has been trained to lie down at his master's word? It may well be that we have every obligation toward helping a child to *want* to worship God, but we have no right to fasten upon him a fixed habit of being in a certain place at a certain time. Such a statement is full of dangers, and needs to be regarded critically, but it also carries implications of a profound truth.

There are yet other considerations against the Family Pew. A minor one, perhaps, is the fact that the presence of little children sometimes disturbs the worship of both the parents and others who may chance to be sitting near by. It may seem heartless—and even Pharisaical—to raise this point, and yet many people know from experience how true it is. However, there is a more weighty consideration—this time on the children's behalf! Is there any likelihood that the regular inclusion of little children in an adult service of worship may have the effect of associating religion in their minds with the unintelligible, the unreal, the unnatural? Suppose that Sunday after Sunday religion assumes the form of hymns which they cannot understand, of a symbolism which is beyond them, of a liturgy into whose experiences they cannot enter for ten or twenty more years, of a sermon which deals with issues they have never faced and in words which they cannot comprehend—what is such an experience, oft repeated, likely to do to children? It may, to be sure, do them much good; but are there not also possibilities of harm within it? It is difficult to say how much unlearning and relearning some of us have had to do because of the early linking of religion in our lives with unreality.

These are some of the reasons both for and against the Family Pew. Unfortunately, we have little of what one might call carefully assembled evidence on the matter. It may be well, therefore, to introduce at this point the findings secured by one person who did make at least the beginning of an effort to discover some facts concerning the effect of the Family Pew. The results of his study are by no means conclusive one way or the other, but they indicate lines along which fruitful inquiry might well be made. The method he followed was to ask a number of questions of several hundred lay people who are at present active in various churches. The more important questions asked and the answers he received are as follows:

"Did your family observe the Family-Pew idea when you were a child? What did you do during the service (draw pictures, read Sunday school papers, etc.)?" To the first question 124 answered "Yes"; 101 answered "No." To the second question he received a variety of replies, which indicated many strange ways of spending the time during this hour of supposed worship.

"If you attended church as a child, was it willingly or because your parents wanted you to attend?" One hundred replied that they had attended willingly; 94 that they had attended under compulsion; 26 answered simply that it was the thing to do.

"Can you remember having had a fine worship experience in the church as a child?" Here the answers are rather disconcerting. Only 59 answered "Yes," while 108 answered "No." Does this mean that the 108 had actually worshiped on many occasions but are scarcely able now to put their fingers on any definite memories of true worship, or should it be taken to mean that their childhood experiences in the church service were not primarily experiences of worship?

"As a child which did you enjoy more—the church-school service or the church service?" Here, perhaps, the emphasis is on the word "enjoy." When the question is put in this fashion, the answers come in clearly on the one side. Two hundred and fifteen answered "the church school" as against a mere 11 who specified "the church." Do these replies throw any light on poor church attendance in adulthood?

"Do you think that a separate junior service in some other part of the church building each Sunday would meet the religious needs of a child until confirmation age?" Here the replies are rather astounding, and by no means consistent with the answers to the next question. To this present question 177 replied "Yes"; 51 "No."

"From your experiences as a child in the church, do you think it better that a child remain away from regular church services until he joins the church?" When confronted with the issue thus baldly, only 36 felt they ought to say "Yes," as compared with 174 who said "No."

"If a condition arose whereby a child were offered the alternative of attending either the church school or the church services (it would not be possible to attend both), which would you advise?" Now the issue is presented in a somewhat different light. Viewing the matter from this angle of the relative value of the two services or programs, 191 favored the church school; 25 the church; and 11 stated that they had no preference.

This admittedly leaves the problem in a confused state, but perhaps this is where it ought to be left at our present level of knowledge. We simply do not know whether we ought to urge the Family Pew on our people strongly, or not.

There is another plan—a sort of variant of the Family-Pew idea—which has had a considerable vogue in recent years, and accordingly deserves separate consideration. It commonly goes by the name of the *Junior Congregation,* or the *Junior Sermon* plan. Its details are probably familiar to all. The children below church-membership age are encouraged to attend the morning church service by the prospect of a brief sermon designed especially for them. As a rule, they sit in a body rather than with their parents scattered throughout the auditorium. They remain through the opening part of the service, which sometimes is adjusted somewhat to their presence and sometimes goes on its way as though there were no children present. At an appropriate point just before the adult sermon there is a five- or ten-minute talk to the children, followed by a hymn which serves for the children as a recessional and in the course of which they make their departure.

Does this plan, now, solve our problem? Does it promise to start the little people of a church on the long road to loyal and effective churchmanship? And does it accomplish this without any present hurt to them or to the service of worship? There can be no doubt that this plan sidesteps artfully several of the chief difficulties which beset the Family Pew, wherein children sit throughout the whole of the morning service. For now the children are released at the end of, say, half an hour. Furthermore, during that time there has been at least one part of the service which was peculiarly their own. All in all, it looks very much as though this plan has solved the problem beautifully.

However, on second thought, a number of rather insistent question marks put in their appearance. Can the Junior Sermon and the recessional be so handled as to avoid interrupting the sequence and the mood of true worship? Again, this plan proceeds on the assumption that it is the adult sermon which is most likely to be beyond the grasp of the children. Is this point well taken? It would be rather ironical—would it not?—if this plan actually succeeded in dismissing the children for the half-hour which they could appreciate best and holding them for the half-hour which was farthest over their heads! Yet this may be the case—especially in a liturgical service. For in such a service the opening part of the hour takes the worshipers through the successive stages of a sense of overwhelming guilt, and the assurance of pardon, and then an outburst of gratitude and joy. Is this the path which little feet would naturally follow to the throne of grace—guilt, and pardon, and joy at the sense of sins forgiven? And the chants and responses which make up the forepart of a liturgical service—they may be far harder to understand than the unpretentious sermons of a kindly pastor. There is no assurance, then, especially in liturgical churches, that the Junior Sermon plan succeeds in eliminating the children from the harder part of the service.

Besides these considerations there are some counts to be brought against the Junior Sermon itself. In the course of time it has fallen into certain rather definite patterns—not all of which are likely to be helpful to children. Generally speaking, the Junior Sermons that are preached fall into one of three categories. There is, first of all, the story-sermon, the body of which is simply a story from the Bible or elsewhere. If the story is a good one, dealing helpfully with matters close to the everyday experiences of children and presenting some fine truth "drawn out in living characters," it may do much good. Secondly, there is the sermon which is nothing more nor less than a heart-to-heart talk by a minister to the children of his parish. On Mother's Day he might talk to them thus about the ways in which children can make mother happy. Whatever the subject, he endeavors to talk helpfully and naturally as he would to the children in his own home. The third type is the parable or object-lesson sermon, and it is this type which needs to be watched most carefully. This is the sermon which uses a string of electric-light bulbs to represent the manner in which our lives light up when they are connected with the power of God; or which speaks of cutting corners instead of going the hard way around and then proceeds to apply this notion to cheating in an examination, and the like. It would not be far wrong to call this type of sermon treacherous, because it seems to be succeeding when it is not. There sit the children in rapt attention! They look for all the world as though they are being indelibly impressed with the deeper meanings of the sermon. But, unless they have a mental age of twelve or over, the chances are that they are not. They see the electric-light bulbs and the electricity, but they do not see at all individual lives and the power of God. They get the point that cutting across actual corners is hard on the grass, but they do not apply this physical truth to such an ethical issue as cheating in an examination. The adults, on the other hand, not only enjoy such sermons but may profit from them greatly. We remember that Jesus told His great parables to adults; there is no record that He told any parables to the children who climbed upon His lap.

It appears, then, that the *Junior Sermon* plan is not a perfect solution—no more than is the *Family Pew*. The *Graded Church* solution is not perfect; it secures for each age-group an experience of worship on its own level but at a costly sacrifice of congregational unity. The *Unified Service* solution is not perfect; it preserves congregational unity beyond a doubt, but at the cost ofttimes of trapping children into attending a service which is alien to their religious experience. In truth, there are no perfect solutions of this difficult problem. All we can hope to do is to cast about for plans which carry with them as many advantages and as few disadvantages as possible.

There is a plan, as yet untried in most part but with some little experience behind it, which looks as though it might dodge a good many difficulties and yet accomplish reasonably well the purpose which we have set before us—namely, that of beginning in childhood to acquaint people with the services of the church. We are thinking now solely of the children under church-membership age. *Why might we not undertake to bring these children into the church service not every Sunday—not even for a part of the service—but five or six times during the year?* There are at least that many times during the year when the presence of children together with the adults is as natural as the gathering of the members of a family at the fireside for family devotions. There is Mother's Day, for example. All people from the tiniest tot to the oldest saint of the congregation know from personal experiences the blessedness of a mother's love and care. On this day, age matters less than usually. Much the same logic applies to Thanksgiving Sunday. All alike have been the beneficiaries of sunshine and rain, seedtime and harvest, friendship and love and beauty, and on this day parent and child can sing side by side, "Now thank we all our God." And likewise of Children's Day, and the Sunday nearest Christmas, and others. On Sundays such as these the children can with im-

146

measurable benefit become a true part of a worshiping congregation. It may well be that a half dozen such Sundays with the tang of reality about them can do more to foster a genuine love for the church and its services than a whole year of routine attendance.

And what of the other Sundays of the year? On those Sundays let the children have an opportunity to worship their Father in heaven in their own separate services and in the language of childhood. Let them grow in such experience until worship is an indispensable part of their lives—a fellowship of the soul with God which they cannot do without! Who shall say that they will not turn regularly to the services of the church for the satisfaction of this hunger when they become men and women? A hunger of the soul is just as impelling as a habit, and more noble.

Treating Children as Members of the Church Family

It has been pointed out time and again, by Christian educators and others, that a church may well be thought of as a family. Like a normal family it includes people of all ages from grandparents to grandchildren. Like a family also it should be marked by a spirit of mutual thoughtfulness and concern for one another's welfare with a special tenderness toward the youngest and most helpless.

This likeness of a church to a family has a decided bearing upon training the young into churchmanship. For it is only as a church maintains the family pattern and the family spirit, especially in its dealings with its children, that it can entertain any hope whatsoever of their growing up into loyal and faithful church members. What family is there which would attempt to win its children by scheduling a class on the subject? No, in the final analysis children can be won to the church and to churchmanship only by treating them as true members of the church family. What does this mean, and how can it be done?

If children are truly members of the church family, they have a perfect right to visit the church auditorium, to use it properly, and to regard it as belonging in part to them. They have no right to play hide-and-seek in it, just as they have no right to dance a jig on the grand piano at home, but it is theirs to use properly. If it is beautiful and rich in symbolism, they can be taken to it on occasion when no one else is there in order to learn something of its meaning and drink in something of its beauty. Furthermore, it is theirs to have services in of their very own. It is interesting to note the variety of ways in which ministers are contriving to hold children's services in the church sanctuary. One minister takes his Juniors to the sanctuary for a monthly service of quiet worship during the first part of the church-school hour. One of the great churches of New York City, which a decade ago was holding services of worship for Juniors and Intermediates in the gymnasiums of the parish hall, now repairs for this purpose to the most worshipful part of the whole building—the sanctuary itself.

Similarly, if children are truly members of the church family, *they have a right to share in the support of the church.* Children ought to have a part in the upkeep and maintenance of a home, even if it be only to put toys away or wash the dishes occasionally. It is essential for both them and the home that they do so! The application of this same principle to the church would seem to be sound beyond a question.

In terms of finances, this implies that children should be allowed to contribute to the church—not to the church school, but to the church—from their earliest years. There are duplex envelopes, attractively adorned with colored pictures, to fit the chubby hand of a very tiny churchman. He may, perhaps, give his envelope to his church-school teacher, but it is meant for the church—and into the church treasury it actually goes. When the Every-Member Canvassers call upon his father and mother to receive their pledges for the support of the church, he makes his too. The causes of the Church at home and abroad are explained to him, in a measure at least, until they become his causes. When he subsequently makes his offering, it may be inconsequential from a financial standpoint but from a higher point of view it is full of meaning. It means that one little fellow is well on the way toward churchmanship.

Again, if children are truly members of the church family, *they have a right to join with all the other members of the family in social fellowship* on occasion. Here too the analogy of the family holds! A mother and a father do not want to spend every free hour with their children, nor are the children any more anxious to be tagging constantly at the heels of their parents. Nevertheless, in a healthy, wholesome family all the members alike will want to enjoy part of their good times together. In the church too there is every reason for occasional social events in which the age-limits are merely the cradle and the grave, and all between those two extremes are welcome.

But, if the children are truly members of the church family, *they have a right not only to play with the other members of the family but to work with them*

149

as well. It is not always easy to include the children in the serious undertakings of a church. Nor is it in a home for that matter! A father mowing a lawn may laughingly protest that with his young son's help it takes him only twice the time that it would otherwise. Yet this experience of working together may be very precious in later years to both father and son. Again, the analogy fits the church. A congregation may set itself to some difficult task. It may undertake to erect a new church building, or to assemble a supply of food for an orphanage, or to root out some community evil. The temptation is great to leave the children out of plans such as these. What real contribution can they make? The truth would seem to be that, while the children may indeed have little to contribute to the project, the project may have a great deal to contribute to the children. Their experience of sharing in this undertaking of the church may go far toward making it their church.

And, finally, if the children are truly members of the church family, *they have a right to be genuinely cared for by the church,* and to know that they are cared for. Modern psychology has a great deal to say about the tragic suspicion, to which children are often subject, that they are unwanted. Sometimes they feel unwanted, even when they are not. Children are highly sensitive creatures. If they are really unwanted, no amount of dissembling on the part of the parents can hide that fact from them. So is it with the church.

Perhaps, then, the problem of training for church membership comes to this in the final analysis: the finest way for a family to win its children to worthy home membership is to love them wisely and share its life with them wherever possible; similarly, the finest

150

way of all for a congregation to win its children to
worthy church membership is to love them wisely and
share its life with them wherever possible. On these
commandments hang all the law and prophets.

VII

THE MINISTER AND HIS YOUNG PEOPLE

THERE is at least one point in the whole field of work with young people concerning which there can be no doubt, and that is the supreme importance of such work. The case is absolutely clear.

To begin with, *the very continuance of the church depends upon our ability to hold our young people.* These restless years (12-23 inclusive) are precisely the years when the danger of loss from the church is greatest. Before this time the danger is not great. Little children are a rather uncritical lot. And after this time of youth is over, the danger of loss is not so great. In adulthood life has settled down to an even keel. Those who have remained in the church thus long are rather likely to remain unto the end. Youth, then, is the Golden Age for leaving the church and its auxiliaries. If this seem too strong a statement, consider a few statistics. A certain denomination reported recently at the end of a year that there were 36,196 Juniors (ages 9-11) in its church schools. At the same time it reported only 32,518 Intermediates (ages 12-14). There should by all logic be as many Intermediates as Juniors in the church schools of a denomination. But the end is not yet! There were at this same time 26,576 Seniors (ages 15-17). And there were only 32,042 Young People (ages 18-23). If all the Juniors of some years back had been kept, there would have been 72,000 instead of 32,000 in the Young People's Department. Where were the other 40,000? Some of them, perhaps, were away at college and thus lost temporarily—or is it permanently?—to the church school, but not 40,000! Some probably had "outgrown" church school and were affiliated now with the church proper, but scarcely 40,000 of them! Where were the rest? And what do figures such as these mean for the future of a denomination?

This single consideration might well be sufficient to underline heavily the supreme importance of a minister's lavishing time and thought and prayer upon his young people. However, there are other valid considerations also. *What of the young people themselves? Is there any time in life when individuals stand more in need of the ministrations of religion than in adolescence?* The years of twelve to twenty-three constitute the most important "becoming" period of all life. An individual enters them as a child; he comes out a full-grown man or woman. He enters them single; he comes out married or well on the way toward marriage. He enters them without a vocation or scarcely a serious thought of one; he comes out, normally, established in his lifework. He enters them as a mere candidate for personality, drawing not only food and shelter but also the very ideals of life from parents and older friends; he comes out with a life-philosophy of his own—good, bad, or indifferent. It is during these years that the three great choices of life are normally made—a lifework, a life-mate, and a life-philosophy. How important it is that during these crucial years an individual should find a minister of the Christian religion constantly at his right-hand! And what a tragedy if he be lost to the church during these crucial years! No return to religion on his part in later life can quite compensate for this loss.

But there is yet another and more subtle reason why work with young people is so richly deserving of a minister's attention. It frequently happens in church work that *there are accomplishments which seem almost impossible when approached with any other age-group, but quite within reach when approached with young people*. Take, for example, the problem of disseminating a reverent yet thoroughly modern view of the Bible. Such a view has been taught in a number of American seminaries for several generations, yet it is still unwelcome in large sections of Protestantism. Ministers go out from these seminaries year after year, thoroughly committed to the historico-critical approach to the Bible. They go into congregations where such a view is anathema. Where shall their teaching begin? It seems hopeless in many congregations to begin it with adults. They are so fixed in their modes of thought that they can be changed only with the greatest difficulty. And it seems almost equally hopeless to begin with children. They are almost sure to carry home badly garbled accounts with deplorable results to the unity of the congregation and the prestige of the minister. But approach this same problem, now, with young people. They are young enough to be malleable; they are old enough to stand on their own feet intellectually and to exercise reasonable discretion in the comments they make at home and elsewhere. It may be that in young people lies our only hope of disseminating what seems to many of us to be a true and invaluable conception of the Bible. The same might be said of a Christian view of economics, or higher standards of church music, or almost any teaching which is at variance with long-accepted custom. Young people, then, are a solvent for insoluble ministerial problems. We ought to be devoutly thankful for young people. Our loss would be inestimable if children became adults overnight.

From whatever angle one approaches the matter, then, the conviction seems inescapable that a minister ought to spend part of every week in intelligent, sympathetic contacts with his young people. But in the minds of many conscientious pastors this clear impression is balanced by another of almost equal strength—namely, that work with young people is very, very difficult. There may be some point in taking a steady, fearless look at the difficulties which surround church work with youth today. They constitute a formidable list, but nothing is quite so formidable once it has been looked full in the face.

WHAT MAKES YOUNG PEOPLE'S WORK SO HARD?

Since the difficulties to be mentioned are also in part failings, we may well take a leaf from the book of the prophet Amos and begin farthest from home. Let us look first at the times, then at the church, and finally at the minister himself.

There is much in the times and *the temper of the times* to throw difficulties in the way of church work with young people. Several summers ago a teacher in a religious summer camp put to his class the general question, "What obstacles stand in the way of true worship on the part of youth today?" He fully expected a series of commonplace answers, such as "poor hymnals," "dingy auditorium," and the like. Imagine his surprise when one of the keenest members of the class replied, "Hard-boiled cynicism!" This chance remark may contain much truth. If young people are truly cynical, they learned their cynicism, of course, from their elders; but could it be that young people are somewhat more sensitive to currents of thought and mood than their elders are? If there is abroad a certain cynicism, a feeling that perhaps nothing is really worth while and that it is not quite fashionable to give oneself fully to any beliefs or ideals whatsoever, this mood passes harmlessly over the heads of many older people who have been firmly grounded in an opposite conviction. But is it so with youth? Do they not respond almost fanatically to the latest fashion in ties and hats? And if ties and hats, why not moods and ideologies? Perhaps, then, young people excel their elders in susceptibility to the currents of cynicism, materialism, secularism, pleasure at any price which are abroad today. And every last one of these is almost the exact antithesis of Christianity! If youth is sometimes deaf to the call of the church, here is one of the reasons.

Furthermore, *the present world is so full of a number of things* for young people to do. We have in mind not only the wide variety of amusements which clamor for their attention, but also the claims made upon their time by the public school and other valuable agencies. Not long ago a group of ministers were discussing the wisest age for holding the church-membership class. One minister reported as his own experience that he found it necessary to hold the class and get it safely out of the way before his young people came into senior high school, because thereafter both their time and their attention were pre-empted by the affairs of the school. A recent account from a near-by city corroborates this point. In this city the public-school system has had to free one night of the week

from extracurricular activities as well as home assignments in order that the churches might have a chance
at their young people.

Worthy of special mention in this evaluation of the
times is *the growing secularization of Sunday.* One
need not be a Puritan to deplore the variety of uses—
some nonreligious and even irreligious—to which the
one day which has long been the special property of
the church is now being put. If it is not a question
of morals, it is at least a question of hours and minutes.
The church, like every other institution, needs a certain amount of mere time in order to get at people
properly. And even when present-day young people
do devote a part of Sunday to the services of the
church, they are often so fagged out by the affairs of
Saturday night that they are utterly unfit either to
worship or to study properly. It is a great pity that
the one day which is set apart for religious purposes
should follow immediately upon the social high-spot
of the week. Perhaps the ancient Hebrews were not
far wrong, after all, in ordaining that the observance
of the Sabbath should begin at sunset of the preceding
day.

One more aspect of the times has a marked bearing
upon our work with youth—namely, *the rapidly growing number of young people who leave home and the
home church around the age of eighteen to go to college.* From the standpoint of church work with youth
such a severing of church relationships is a near-trag-
edy, particularly when it is remembered that those
who leave in this manner are usually the ablest in the
community, the leaders of tomorrow. Eighteen is
about the worst possible age at which to break church
ties. And, in spite of the ofttimes heroic efforts of

college pastors and churches in college communities, there is no assurance that new ties are formed in sufficient measure to replace the old. Some years ago a study was made of the church affiliations of some 1,600 students on the campus of a major university. It was found that in their home churches about half of these students had been connected with a church school, and about 40 per cent with a young people's society. During the university years these percentages dropped to 5 per cent and 10 per cent respectively.[1] It is doubtful whether the religious activities of the campus compensate for this loss. If not, this is a situation which may rightly be called serious.

But to come a little closer home, not all of the obstacles to effective work with young people originate in the world outside the Church. Some high barriers between youth and the Church have been raised by the Church itself—never intentionally, of course. Perhaps the heart of the difficulty is that *the Church throughout its long history has been in the main adult-centered.* It has been governed by adults. Its creeds have been written by adults. Its hymns have been composed by adults. It has thought adult thoughts, stressed adult interests, viewed the world through adult eyes—and then wondered why young people did not rush into its fold! Perhaps it could not have done otherwise, but its adult-orientation has certainly made its way harder with youth. Consider, for example, the theological controversies which fill so many chapters in church history! What do these mean to young people? Or the hymns of the Church! Let a minister read them

---

[1] *Religious Education*, 1928, pp. 917ff. "Religious Attitudes and Activities of University Students: A Report," by George H. Betts.

over one by one to a healthy group of sixteen-year-
olds. How many of them strike fire? Yet these same
sixteen-year-olds are expected to attend church regularly. Even the great symbolic rituals of the Church
stoop but seldom to the level of young people's interests and understanding. Young people love ritual—
a candle-lighting service, for example—but it must
speak a language which they can comprehend and
appreciate. Something might be said here also concerning sermons and orders of worship, but these will
be dealt with later. Not at all in a spirit of faultfind-
ing but merely as a statement of fact it can be said in
short that youth find much that the Church says and
does rather irrelevant to their lives. In the study previously reported, the university students were asked
to give their reasons for failing to attend church. The
reason which ranked second in importance in their
answers was to the effect that the church was not helpful.[2]

It is possible to play a number of variations on this
major theme of the adult-centeredness of the Church.
One of these might well stress the point that *the Christian way of life has often been presented to young
people in terms predominantly negative.* In order
to be Christians they are told they must give up this,
and sacrifice that. What a queer way to win youth to
the Church! It is as if a suitor should try to win his
lady by the questionable device of expounding to her
the joys she must give up when she casts in her lot
with his. It is most instructive to note that the religious youth program which has gone farthest toward
capturing the imagination of the young people of
America has had as its central theme "Christian Youth

---

[2] *Ibid.*

Building a New World." There is challenge in that. There is sacrifice also, but sacrifice for a purpose— not mere negation.

Perhaps it is saying the same thing in different words to point out that *the Church has often been less than sympathetic to the natural desire of young people for amusement.* Dancing is a case in point. A church-school teacher said recently that there was no use of discussing dancing with her class of young people. They would not say what they truly thought about the matter, but merely what they felt they were expected to say. In other words, they had lost all faith in the willingness of the Church to hear them open-mindedly. This is not to imply that a church ought necessarily to permit dancing within its buildings, or even that it ought to condone dancing in general. All that it implies is the obligation of the Church to meet young people on common ground and prove to them beyond a doubt that it is honestly trying to see life through their eyes. Such a Church youth will trust and love, even if it forbids at times what they want to do.

In our own day a new barrier rises high between some churches and their young people—*a barrier of doctrinal difference.* We stand between two worlds today, doctrinally speaking. Many of our youth, especially those who have gone to college, have moved over into the new world—a world dominated by the scientific temper. Not a few churches still inhabit the old world, and do so in all sincerity. The point is that it is the young people who suffer most from such a state of affairs. They are like immigrants in a new country. Often their thoughts turn longingly toward the homeland, but they cannot go back. They now live in a new world, speak a new language, think new thoughts, and the ideas and customs of the old world are sometimes actually repulsive to them. A pastor spoke recently with heavy heart of a young man of his congregation who had been at one time an ardent worker in his church. Then he went to college (a mere stone's throw away). He seems interested in the church no longer. The pastor was inclined to blame the college for this defection, and the college may indeed have handled the transition from the old world to the new rather badly. However, it is fair to ask whether part of the responsibility does not fall back upon the home church. What has it done to see life through the eyes of this young man? Has it a right to go on indefinitely proclaiming beliefs which repel him and his kind without a heart-searching examination of those beliefs in the light of all the tested knowledge available? It may be forced to pay a heavy price, if it insists on so doing.

It will perhaps not appear too ungracious to add that *certain features in the practical ordering of the Church's life* have also had the effect of alienating the affections of youth. For one thing, the Church has not always been happy in the choice of leaders for young people. It has given them teachers but little older than themselves. Or it has offered them teachers old in age and in spirit, whose chief qualifications were a knowledge of the Bible and a beautiful earnestness of purpose. Or it has left young people's societies to struggle along without any mature leadership whatsoever. Again, young people have not always been grouped into classes and departments and societies with proper care. It must be remembered that they are keenly sensitive to age-differences—much more so than adults. The gap between twelve and eighteen is ten times wider than that between fifty-two and fifty-eight. We should probably be surprised to discover how many youth have been lost to the church because of poor grouping. In a certain church school a number of young women were at the right age for promotion to the Adult Department. However, the only class provided for them belonged to another generation (it included the aunt of a member of the younger class). The young women rebelled, and stated in terms which all might understand that under those conditions they would come to church school no more. It is difficult to blame them too harshly. And, finally, the church has been more successful in finding work for youth in the auxiliaries than in the church proper. Is it any wonder, then, that they feel closer to the auxiliaries than they do to the church? Some striking statistics on this point are given by Doctor Munro.[3] A number of youth delegates in summer conferences were asked to list the offices which they held in their home churches. Upon classification it was found that they occupied in all 294 positions of responsibility in auxiliary organizations as compared with only 18 in the church proper—a ratio of about 16 to 1. It would not be surprising if their loyalties were distributed in about the same ratio.

To come at last to *the minister himself,* most men in the profession would probably confess freely that they too must be constantly on their guard against the taint of adult-centeredness. In their preaching, in their praying, in their planning, it is easier for them to think of adults than of youth. For the minister is himself

---

[3] Munro, H. C., *The Pastor and Religious Education.* The Abingdon Press, 1930, p. 53.

an adult. He sees life through the eyes of adults. His natural fellowship is with adults. His salary comes largely from adults. His training has fitted him in all likelihood for a ministry mainly to adults. It is only by an heroic spiritual effort that a minister can regard himself as the pastor of young people as well as the pastor of adults. And the older and more experienced a minister becomes, the higher the barrier tends to grow between himself and his young people. At the outset of his ministry, it is easy enough for him to understand them, and they him, but he is in all other respects unfitted as yet to give them the maximum help. As the years go by his Christian experience grows, his personality ripens and develops, his wisdom in dealing with people and with organizations increases, and his general usefulness in the ministry multiplies rapidly. But the very years which accomplish these changes also remove him farther from his own youth and from youth in general. Thus it is that when he is best fitted in point of age to understand young people, he is least able to give them help; and when he is most able to give them help, he is least fitted by age to understand them. It seems as though everything conspires together to hamper a minister's work with his young people.

Considering all these obstacles, the temptation is keen to give it up largely, or at least to give it over to youth organizations and their lay-leaders with a sigh of regret and one last look in the mirror at the tell-tale gray above the temples. But to do so is to abandon one of the most rewarding phases of the whole Christian ministry. There is no more responsive congregation imaginable than, say, a group of senior-high-school boys and girls. They are so honest, so frank, and so quick to rise with all the vigor of their youth to an idealistic challenge! Truly, of such is the kingdom of heaven.

That is why so many ministers today are girding up their loins and, with a laugh at all the difficulties, setting themselves to one of the most worth-while tasks in the Christian ministry—work with young people. There would seem to be three chief ways in which the average minister reaches youth: first, through the regular services of the church; secondly, through the youth organizations which are set up in his parish; and, finally, through friendly, personal contacts with them as individuals.

Young People and the Church Service

What can a minister do to get his young people to attend church regularly? And—more important still —what can he do to guarantee that they will receive real spiritual benefit when they do attend? These questions lie close to the heart of every faithful pastor.

A number of answers suggest themselves. We have spoken elsewhere of the desirability of shortening the church-school worship service, so that youth as well as their elders will come to look to the morning church service as the proper time and place for worship. This is all to the good, and needs to be done. However, it merely removes an obstacle to church attendance. It opens a door, but affords no assurance that young people will enter.

Some ministers follow the plan of encouraging church-school classes to attend church occasionally in a body. A special appeal is made on a given Sunday for a large attendance at church, and due recognition is given the class or classes in the church service. Even if this works for the time being, it does not get to the root of the matter. Like all special plans and devices, it is merely an expedient which offers no permanent solution.

Another answer—and a far sounder one—places reliance mainly in *a thorough discussion with young people of the subject of worship,* in the hope that they will come to appreciate worship and its place in life and conceive a desire for experiencing true worship regularly. Such a discussion may include some sharpening of their concept of God, some clarification also of what prayer is and does, an analysis of their own worship-experiences and the values derived therefrom, as well as a study of the particular order of service in use in the church in question. This last-named item is doubly necessary for a liturgical service. There is a psychological sequence in such a service which is probably lost on most young people. A bit of evidence on this point will be given at a later point in this discussion. Suffice it here to say that a minister's son who had grown up with a semiliturgical service once testified that he had sung the *Gloria in Excelsis* once a Sunday since childhood with no idea whatsoever why it was introduced into the service exactly where it was. Incidentally, a fascinating way of interpreting a liturgical service is to parallel its steps with the experience of the young Isaiah in the temple "in the year that king Uzziah died." The parallel is almost perfect! Here, then, is one sound solution to the problem before us.

Another valid solution is to *hunt for ways of giving young people a share in the service.* However, the rub comes in finding suitable ways for such participation without violating the conventions which have grown up around this hour. Here, obviously, the church school enjoys a decided advantage over the church, and for this very reason it so often wins out in the competition for young people's loyalties. The contest is really not a fair one at all. There are countless ways in which youth can share in the church-school hour. Broadly speaking, there are only three points at which they can be admitted ordinarily to the church services: ushering, singing in the choir, and conducting an evening service on occasion. Simply because they are so few these three opportunities ought to be exploited to the utmost. Ushering might well be made a permanent possession of youth. There can be chorus choirs (which some music schools today prefer to the paid quartet), and Junior choirs, and Intermediate choirs—and all without detriment to the service of worship, but, rather, the contrary. And as for the evening service—that seems to be made to order for occasional conduct by young people. In addition to services of the usual type they can prepare and conduct dramatic services, musical services, observances of special days, and symbolic rituals such as a candle-lighting service. Only there is one caution to be sounded! Unless the young people are unusually competent, it is essential that the minister or some other qualified person coach them painstakingly during their preparation for the service. It will not do for a minister to turn over a Sunday evening to his young people, and then wash his hands of the matter. That is to invite almost certain failure, and prejudice the whole experiment. With proper guidance they will offer a service which is a credit to them and a blessing to those who attend.

Without depreciating the worth of the foregoing

solutions to our problem, the suspicion still remains that they do not get to the heart of the matter. *The basic question is still untouched: Is the church service, including sermon and all, suited to young people?* Is it meaningful to them? Does it speak their language? Do hymns, Scriptures, and prayers appeal to them deeply? Does the order of worship correspond at all to the rhythm of their own religious experience? Is the sermon spiritually helpful to them? Is the entire service an open highway between them and the Almighty? Until these questions can be answered largely in the affirmative, the problem of young people and the church service will not be met—no matter what else we do.

It may be valuable to note at this point what some young people and young adults actually think about worship in general and the church service in particular. A questionnaire was given to about 170 persons between the ages of 15 and 34, one third of whom were delegates at a summer religious camp and the remainder merely members of average congregations. Some of the following questions and answers contain much food for thought for ministers:

"Do you like a read prayer or a free prayer better in a church service?" The answers here were astounding. One hundred and fifty-one favored the free prayer; 7 the read prayer; and 7 liked both equally well. The person making the investigation goes on to say that so far as he can discern there was no connection between the answers given and what the respondents were accustomed to in their home churches. In fact, most of them were accustomed to both types of prayer. These replies raise a question which refuses to be put down: Are the liturgies which are in use in many Protestant churches suitable vehicles of worship for young people?

"In which of the elements of the worship service (music, prayer, Scripture, sermon, etc.) are you the most likely to be led into true worship?" The replies mentioned prayer 88 times, the sermon 67 times, music 60 times, Scripture 6 times, and silence 5 times. The first thing to strike one's eye in these answers is the very slight worship-value of the Scripture lessons. These purport to be the very word of God to man; and yet almost uniformly they fail to engender the experience of worship. What could we do to enhance the worship value of the Scripture readings in our services? Another surprising fact is that silence was mentioned 5 times—surprising because there is so little silence in the average Protestant service to serve as a basis of judgment. Apparently, it is appreciated. Perhaps we ought to make more use of it.

"Comment on whether you worship more readily in the conventional places (church, auditorium, chapel, etc.) or in natural surroundings." Here the line of division is sharply drawn between the campers and the noncampers. Of the former 47 specified natural surroundings, 5 the conventional, and 6 both. Among the latter the proportion is reversed. Only 21 preferred the natural surroundings, 74 the conventional, and 10 both. Apparently, nature is an open road to God for all young people who have had a chance to take it. Have we made full use of it in our church services? Would it be possible to have several services each year in the out-of-doors? Could the nature references in our regular services be more abundant?

"Have you ever really worshiped? If so, mention several occasions when you have, and tell why you think you really worshiped on these occasions." The investigator cites a number of replies to this question. It will have to suffice here to give several of those listed. The amazing thing to note in these is that not a single one gives any indication of ever having worshiped in a church service.

"I worshiped in the sanctuary of my home church, when I sat there alone faintly hearing the singing of 'Lord, in this Thy mercy's day' by the young people's society in another part of the church. Also last Christmas Eve while singing carols out in a driving snowstorm. A large group of young people of the Music Guild went about our city after our Christmas-Eve service. The snow under foot, the large flakes coming down, and the wind—all seemed to blend so perfectly with the music that it was uplifting and inspirational for me, and I realized afterward that I had been worshiping."

"I worshiped the day mother was on the operating-table fighting for her life. I prayed to God to spare her. I truly believe I worshiped because I went to my bedroom and knelt down and prayed for mother. I forgot everything about me; after a while I felt better. A few hours later word came from the hospital that mother would live."

"I have worshiped: (1) Alone in a simply appointed church on a college campus. (2) In the chapel of nature. (3) In a church looking through an open window at the vast panorama of the skies at night. On these occasions I felt in contact with a Divine Being."

Before inquiring further into the meaning of these replies, there may be added to them a reaction received from a group of a dozen Intermediate boys. A special effort had been put forth over a period of three months to secure their attendance at the morning church service. At the close of this period they were asked several questions, among which was the following: *"How do you think we are supposed to feel during the first part of the service?"* To this question, 2 of the boys gave no answer; 6 said "reverent"; 2 said "religiously"; 1 said "be in praying mood." In another connection one of the boys voiced his dislike for this part of the service. Now, the point is that this particular church uses a liturgical service, the opening portion of which is designed first to call the worshiper to repentance for his sins and then to grant him the joyful assurance of sins forgiven. To all appearances these boys missed the point entirely, and they may even have resented it a little—half subconsciously.

What, now, is the meaning of all this? How shall we proceed to make the church service as meaningful as possible to young people? It will not do, of course, to lose sight of the older members of the congregation. They have as much right to be considered as those who are younger—but scarcely any more right. If young people are expected to attend the church service, and if they are a true part of the congregation, then it seems to follow that a minister ought to plan his service with an age-span of, say, fifteen to seventy in his mind's eye. But what can he do?

One answer is that in the choosing of his hymns and Scripture readings he might summon in imagination a man of seventy and a boy of fifteen to sit before him as a Board of Censors. Each hymn is submitted in silence to this board; each Scripture passage; and each prayer. The boy of fifteen has no right to expect that *every* hymn, *every* Scripture, *every* paragraph of a prayer be fully significant to him. But if there are too many hymns about heaven, he has a right to object. If too many of the Scripture readings are chosen from difficult passages in the Epistles, he has a right to object. And if too many of the prayers carry to the Lord concerns of full-grown men and women only, he has a right to object.

But what of the liturgical service? This is the hardest question of all. For the liturgical service—for all its beauty, dignity, and orderliness—is frequently laden down with materials which young people find hard to understand and to which, it seems, they do not always respond kindly. Its phraseology is that of three or four hundred years ago. Its responses have the flavor of another world and another age about them. These very characteristics, to be sure, spell the liturgy's strength; but to some young people they seem to be a stumbling-block—a hindrance rather than an aid to true worship. Furthermore, the typical liturgy lays heavy stress during the early part of the worship hour upon sin and guilt. It often includes a Call to Confession, a joint Confession, the singing of the beautiful but doleful Kyrie, and the Declaration of Pardon. Consider all this from the standpoint of youth. Is this native to their religious experience? Is this the normal way for them to approach the Heavenly Father? There are indeed a number of young people who are oppressed by a heavy sense of guilt, but this reflects rather commonly a morbid consciousness of sex offenses, either real or imagined, and is by no means to be encouraged. It is doubtful whether many normal young people, if left to themselves, would construct a worship service whose early stages were heavily burdened with a sense of guilt.

If this criticism is at all sound, something should be done—but what? The service can, of course, be interpreted carefully to young people, as previously suggested. It may even be simplified at points. But perhaps more heroic treatment still is needed. We may be forced to revise our Protestant liturgies—that is, if we truly want to hold our young people. Such revision could, without sacrificing continuity with the past, strike out obsolete diction and ponderous theological terms. But it could do more. It could provide for some seasons of the church year orders of service which make little or nothing of guilt, but worship the Lord throughout on the high plane of joyous thanksgiving or of solemn dedication to the kingdom of God. There is good reason for believing that many youth— as well as their fathers and mothers—could let their souls go in such services with a reckless abandon which the present liturgies inhibit. Let us hope, then, that the day will come when liturgists will give some real attention to the religious requirements of youth. For surely a living soul is worth as much as a tradition!

But there still remains the sermon, which consumes almost half of the typical Protestant church service. How shall the sermon be made meaningful to youth? Again, we may let the young people themselves speak. The same investigator to whom reference was previously made asked one straightforward question concerning the sermon: *"What in your mind are the characteristics of a good sermon?"* The answers came in pell-mell, and he classified them under several main heads. They are not overly penetrating, but they do help us to see the sermon through the eyes of youth. (For sake of convenience the quotation marks are omitted; the answers of the young people are given, however.)

1. *Relation to the Bible*

> Biblical examples should be used.
> The sermon should be an interpretation of the Bible.
> The sermon should correlate the events of the day with the laws of the Bible.

2. *Subject matter in general*

> Should be fitted to the needs of the congregation.
> Should deal with present-day problems.
> Good and interesting topic.
> One which contains no platitudes.
> Should keep up with a changing world.
> Timeliness.

Examples from everyday life.

Not the "hell-fire and damnation" kind.

Should apply the ideals and principles of Jesus to modern life.

3. *What it should do*

Must give us something useful.

Should help solve personal problems and lead to a larger view of living.

Should teach a lesson.

Should inspire the listeners.

Should "hit" us.

Should challenge us to do something and tell us how to do it.

Should show evils and solutions (plan of action).

4. *Manner of organization and presentation*

Not too long. To the point. Not drawn out. Begin at the beginning and end at the ending.

Common talk.

Clear.

Speaker should be interesting.

Follow the topic through.

Should have several points which are stressed.

Should not be read.

There should be a short summary at the end.

Should be from the heart and touch the heart of the listener.

Sincerity.

Preacher must know what he is talking about.

There must be unity.

Modulations in the preacher's voice.

Not too much action by the preacher.

Must not be over the heads of the people.

Here is a fleeting glimpse of ourselves as others see us. Among these random remarks certain threads of emphasis are plainly visible. These young people want sincerity in the preacher. They are quick to notice and resent undue gesticulation. They much prefer a manner that is quiet, serious, and natural. Their chief demand of the sermon seems to be that it help them in their daily living. They do not care particularly that it be Biblical, although some do mention the Bible. They do not seem at all interested in its being learned. They do not want to be dazzled; they want to be helped. Strangely, they do not seem primarily concerned that it be interesting. They do not plead for illustrations, or anecdotes, or spectacular devices. They do not want to be amused; *they want to be helped*. Furthermore, there is no indication that they desire a preacher to "talk down" to them. They want no juvenile sermon; no story-sermon; no sermon which will avoid all strain upon their intelligence. They do ask for clearness, but, if we can take them at their word, they are more than willing that it be meaty and intellectually worthy. The points which these young people make might constitute a good start toward a science of homiletics for youth. Practically nothing has been written on this subject. It is a science for which there is great need.

There remains one troublesome question in this field of preaching to youth. The average minister must preach not to young people alone, but to young people and adults conjoined in one congregation. This fact complicates the situation tremendously. How shall he deal fairly with both generations? There appear to be only three ways out. On occasion—perhaps rarely—he can focus his sermon on some urgent need of one of the two groups, leaving the other to get out of it what they can. It is easy to see how a preacher desiring to render the maximum help to his people may find it necessary to sharpen his focus in this manner from time to time. Again, there may be some

sermons to which the preacher can give a sort of bi-
focal treatment—that is, he can discuss the theme first
from the standpoint of the older generation and then
from the standpoint of the younger. For example,
in dealing with the subject of the Christian home a
minister might quite naturally view the home and its
problems through the eyes of parents, and then through
the eyes of adolescents, and combine these two views
organically into one sermon of real value. And, finally, there will be many themes so universal in their
character that a single treatment of them will strike
home to both youth and their elders—God, prayer,
sin, salvation, social issues, and a whole similar host.
Subjects such as these mean much the same to all ages.
If such universal themes be handled simply, clearly,
concretely, a high-school boy and his father can sit
side by side in the same pew and derive equal benefit
from the sermon. However, even here the minister
in order to stay on the safe side needs to have both boy
and father in his mind's eye as he prepares his sermon.
If they sit together thus in imagination in the minister's
study, they will be more likely to sit together in church
on the following Sunday, and the Sundays thereafter.

THE MINISTER AND HIS YOUTH ORGANIZATIONS

It is not feasible to go into detail here concerning
matters of organization and method in the youth work
of a church. Excellent books are available on this
subject. It is more to the point here to consider a few
general principles by which a minister may be guided
in all his dealings with the youth organizations of his
church.

One such principle which is receiving wide approval
is that *the more nearly a minister can approximate the*

ideal of a Youth Department of the Church rather than a welter of separate agencies, the better. This does not imply necessarily that there shall be no distinct youth organizations. Indeed, the situation may require several. For one thing, it is next to impossible to include successfully the young people of junior-high-school age (12-14) with those of senior-high-school age and above in joint activities and organizations. The two groups mix little better than oil and water. Many congregations have tried to combine them, but with indifferent success. And there may be other valid reasons for a strictly limited number of youth organizations. Some situations seem to call for the establishment of a Boy Scout troop or a 4-H Club under church auspices. Or, there may be a group keenly interested in missions or dramatics, and therefore eager for a life of its own.

Nevertheless, the principle remains sound. The fewer youth organizations in any church, the better! It may be that there is need for a society of some sort with meetings on Sunday evening, but let the burden of proof rest on those who propose such a society. Is it possible for the young people to have a department of their own in the church school, with their own officers and discussions on topics of their own choice? If so, why have an additional society? If an evening meeting still seems advisable, it can be merely one more session of the Young People's Department of the church school with no extra machinery at all. The same logic applies in the case of a separate missionary agency for youth. If missions can be given a real place in the church-school curriculum so that no separate organization is required, so much the better! For now missionary education will be at the disposal of all the youth of the church, instead of merely the few who have a peculiar interest in this phase of the Christian enterprise.

Thus the Young People's Department of the church school—in our present stage of development, at least— becomes the center of the youth work of a church. Let as much as possible be done through it. Exhaust its possibilities before setting up additional organizations. And, if other agencies seem necessary to meet the needs of youth, let their representatives unite with this department in joint planning. And, further, think and speak of all this as the Youth Department of the Church! The phrase "the young people of our church" ought to appear frequently in announcements and on posters and in the minds of the church people. Such would seem to be the practical meaning of the principle we are considering—for the time being at least. It may have an even larger meaning in the future.

The following is a half-page account of an instance of unified, church-centered youth work. Besides the organization mentioned here, there is no other agency for young people in the church concerned except a Boy Scout troop, which really serves the community more than it serves the church constituency.

In our congregation the various activities of the young people are included in what is known as the "Young People's Department." This is not regarded as an organization separate from the church, but a part of it. Its activities are planned and carried out by the Young People's Council, which is elected by the department twice a year and is formally installed in office. Besides the usual officers, this Council includes the chairmen of the various committees and an adult principal who serves as counselor. The Council meets once a month.

The committees are as follows: (1) The program committee, which arranges for topics and leaders for the Sunday-morning worship service in the Young People's Department of the church school, and also for the Sunday-evening meeting. It is our aim to have the themes of these two services related. (2) The church life committee, which has charge of the pageants presented, and, in short, is responsible for all activities connected with the church as a whole. (3) The social committee, which plans all recreational activities whether indoors or out. (4) The community life committee, which has charge of all activities connected with other organizations in the community. During the past year this committee has arranged several contacts with a Negro church in our city.

Another basic principle which is gaining wide acceptance is that *the more nearly a church's young people can determine their own program (with guidance, of course), the better.* It is fatal merely to accept program suggestions which come down from headquarters—just as fatal as for a minister to have his sermon themes Sunday by Sunday prescribed from an office a thousand miles away.

Of course young people's groups differ vastly in their ability to stand on their own feet. Some have never taken the first tottering steps in the direction of a discriminating use of whatever program suggestions come their way. About all that can be done in such a group at first is to look over with them their materials for the next few months, select the topics or lessons which promise to be worth while, strike out the rest, and fill in the gaps with topics of their own choosing. The units in the "Everyday Adventures for Christian Living" series of The Methodist Book Concern are excellent for this "gap-filling" purpose. As time goes on they will gain in confidence, and rejoice finally in a program which is their own.

The actual work of building a program can best be done at what may be called a "Planning Meeting." This is where the blueprints are drawn for the program that is to be. A worker with young people has described such a Planning Meeting, and has managed to capture something of the youthful spirit which pervaded it. We invite ourselves, therefore, to the meeting.

May 3, 7:30–10:00 P.M. at a home.

Twelve people present: 3 adult teachers; 3 young adult officers; 6 young people representing several Sunday-school classes, the Young People's Fellowship, and the Westminster Guild.

Superintendent leading. Informal—everybody talking and suggesting. Secretary appointed to present findings to the department next Sunday.

Eight items which had grown out of the work week by week were given unnumbered on a slip of paper to each person present. They were taken up in the following order and with the following results:

(1) What is the matter with us? (That is, how can we prevent the usual summer slump?) Discussion: Not much the matter with us; it's with the others who don't come; but how much are we responsible for the disinterested? Decided: To be more friendly; forget self and talk to others each Sunday; talk in terms of what we do well and what went over fine, and leave the rest for private conference.

(2) Recreation during spring and summer. Discussion: What the objectives of this season's recreation should be; suited to everybody's enjoyment (golf and tennis ruled out); suited to season (mainly outdoors); analysis of the times last summer that we liked best; one result to be attained is to draw in those home from college. Decided: To have outdoor scavenger hunt; Mother's Day party; swim at Peach Bottom; outdoor vespers on Sunday once a month; general committee to make specific plans and select subcommittees for each event; Mother's Day

179

party next; general discussion of what would interest the mothers for such a party.

(3) Objectives the department had adopted for the period of January to April. Little discussion needed; pretty well taken care of under other heads.

(4) Questionnaire to find the chief interests of the department. Decided: What items to include; to shoot it through the department next Sunday; to make Robert responsible for completing it.

(5) Evening meetings. Decided: General plan of last year good—namely, speakers and discussion; discontinue for the summer except for monthly vesper service; committee named to plan for this.

(6) Forum: I Believe in Missions vs. I Do Not Believe in Missions. Suggestion for this grew out of current Sunday-school course. Decided: Not a debate; leader selected; one person chosen to start it off on each side; teachers to take notes for follow-up teaching. We spent a profitable half-hour going through materials on hand, looking for telling chapters, incidents, etc., with which each one present loaded up and also took some to give out. (This forum, by the way, worked out very well and gave us plans for worship and teaching sessions for the rest of the quarter.) Decided to have stereopticon pictures in several weeks.

(7) Budget for the coming year. Discussion: Last year's budget; not enough to missions; too much contributed by one individual; not as much needed this year for equipment. Budget adopted: Missions, $50; Equipment (books, etc.), $15; Postage, $10; Recreation, $10; Speakers, slides, etc., $15; Total, $100. To be raised: By gifts; by a play in the fall; recreation to pay for itself by contributions.

(8) Spiritual emphasis. Discussion: We have physical reserves (e.g., playing better than we can in a crisis); need for spiritual reserves; how to accumulate these; why we don't read the Bible more (very illuminating); why we should, and what we should read. Decided: Bible reading agreed upon by all; one boy agreed to read a book of the Bible daily for one week, write his reactions day by day, and report on it at a later worship service on the

theme "How to become more devoted to Christ." (This was a most interesting development of a very worth-while discussion.)

Believe it or not, we had time to sit around and talk until 10:30 or more, and have refreshments, and feel we had moved forward a long way.

The next Sunday Dick had a fine "Findings" report, the Budget was explained and adopted, and committees enlarged to include everybody present on that Sunday as well as others. The plans for the Forum worked out better than we had anticipated because everybody was "in on it" from the beginning.

We did not have prayer at this Planning Meeting. The group gathered helter-skelter as such groups do. The close was on a high note, concerned with very personal matters and devotion to Christ.

Many secrets of good work with young people are hidden away in this spirited account of a Planning Meeting. Here is a truly vital program taking shape under our very eyes.

Under this same head of the importance of "homemade" programs it is worth noting that the finest work is not always done in a regularly organized society or guild with regular meeting times and all-too-regular meetings. Sometimes it is done rather through informal, unconventional groups whose only merit is their vitality and their singleness of purpose. For example, one minister met irregularly with a group of young men who came to his home for the sole purpose of discussing theology, social issues, or whatever came to their minds. There was no constitution, no organization, no study materials—in fact, nothing but a purpose and a fellowship; but it exerted a powerful influence for good over the lives of those young men. To cite another example, an unusually vigorous youth group in a large city exists for the sole purpose of breaking down the barriers between the white and colored races in their city. It seems to have done something for its members that the more conventional youth programs failed to accomplish. Perhaps, after all, it is more essential for a group of young people to be able to say "This one thing I do" than to have an organizational set-up that can be nicely diagrammed on paper.

A third general principle concerns the part a minister ought to take personally in his youth organizations. It may be stated thus: His is the difficult art of giving guidance from the circumference rather than from the center of a youth group. A beautiful example of the practice of this fine art is afforded by the conduct of a certain camp director. He was sitting in one of the meetings of the senate, which was the "student government" organization of the camp. One of the senators made a proposal which could not possibly be made to work, as the director well knew. What should he do? He might have kept silent, but he did not. He might have vetoed the proposal, but he did not. Instead he said: "Let's think a bit about this matter. Have you thought of this? Have you thought of that?" And thus he led them most skillfully to see all that he saw—and of their own accord they dropped the proposal. He did not make the decision for them; and yet, if he had not been there, they would have decided otherwise. This experience hits off admirably the nature of the minister's rôle both in young people's sessions and in smaller meetings for the purpose of laying plans. The young people do not want him to make the plans. They do not want him to appoint the officers. They do not want him or any other adults to make long speeches at their meetings. What they want him to do is to help them see what they would not see without his help; to put his richer experience at their disposal without dictating or "stealing the show." This is one of the finest of the fine arts, and one of the hardest to master. But when proficiency in it finally arrives, the way is at last open into the heart of the youth organizations, and into the hearts of the young people themselves.

THE MINISTER'S PERSONAL RELATIONS WITH YOUNG PEOPLE

This heading might mean either of two things; it probably ought to be allowed to mean both.

In the first place, how shall a minister conduct himself when he is with young people either singly or in a group? Shall he be a "good fellow"? Shall he sing, and laugh, and joke, and play games with them? Or shall he stand on his dignity as a minister, remembering constantly that he is a man of the cloth and an ordained representative of the church?

The opinions of the young people themselves are fairly clear. They do not care particularly for a minister who is very self-consciously a minister and only incidentally a man. In the company of such a person they will wear a constant false front, dressing up their speech and actions for the occasion and then doing what they please when his back is turned. Such a man will never really know his youth and consequently will not be able to help them, for the reason that they will not allow him to know them. They do not care for him. They do not trust him. He simply does not count in their young lives. To all intents and purposes he is an inhabitant of another world.

On the other hand, they do not care for a "slap-'em-on-the-back" hilarity. They are likely to despise a minister who is patently trying to be a good fellow—putting his arms around them, punching them slyly in the ribs, demanding that he be called by his first name, and the like. They know this to be just as unreal as an artificial show of dignity, and in addition rather immature and selfish. For such a minister is in all probability seeking a superficial popularity for himself, rather than a genuine fellowship with his young people to the end that he may live his life into theirs.

Their ideal would seem to be a person who is every inch a minister and at the same time every inch a human being. They want him to be a minister—completely devoted to his high calling and thoroughly proud of it, although saying little about it. They would like him at the same time to be human—perfectly natural, enjoying wholesome sports and pleasures, simply being himself. In fact, their chief advice to him would probably take the slang form, "Be yourself!" Let him play baseball with them and enjoy it to the full, but if he is forty years of age, let him act like forty and not like fifteen. Let him try no juvenile tricks. Let him take no silly pleasure in exhibiting his prowess before them. If he is so fortunate as to knock a two-bagger, let him not try with grimly set jaw to urge his aging legs on to third base. Instead let him be what he really is—a minister of the gospel in middle life who genuinely cares for youth and is at the present moment enjoying fellowship with them on a wholesome plane. A minister can play baseball with a group of young people one hour and lead them in a worship service the next, provided he is himself both times.

But, secondly, what can a minister do by way of giving counsel and guidance to his young parishioners

individually, one by one? For surely it is not enough
to deal with these young people by ten's and twenty's!
They are now face to face with more problems, issues,
and temptations per hour and per day than ever before
or ever again! Often they need desperately someone
with whom to talk. And often they have no one! In
some cases they do not feel free to go to their parents,
or their church-school teachers, or their public-school
teachers, or even their own comrades. They need a
pastor, if anyone does!

The cases that follow are representative of the several types which will come to a pastor's attention, if
he will keep the way open. They run the usual gamut
of adolescent problems—sex, vocation, religious difficulties, and relations with parents. All are actual
cases, altered sufficiently to conceal their identity.

A young man of fine abilities. His fiancée had been
killed. His relation with his father was very unhappy.
He was contemplating suicide.

A young woman with a consuming interest in pulp
magazines, amounting to sexual perversion. She had even
been known to make improper advances to relatives.

A young man who was an adopted child. His foster
parents had never informed him of his adoption. His
first knowledge of it came when he was a child in school.
A schoolmate cruelly cast it up to him that he was not
living with his real parents. At eighteen he was loud and
boisterous, but had no idea why he acted in this manner.

A girl greatly perplexed over who and where God is.
All through childhood she had given no thought to the
matter, accepting without question an immature conception of God. Around fifteen the question was thoroughly
pried open for her. She was grateful for a chance to talk
the matter over with a minister.

A college student attending a summer conference. The
question was put to a class of which he was a member,

"What does religion mean to you?" He answered like a flash: "Fear, doubt, and uncertainty."

A young woman whose mother was dead, and whose father had remarried. Her stepmother was extremely jealous of her. She would not allow her to come into the home on vacations from college, or at best very grudgingly. The young woman was greatly distressed over the situation.

An older adolescent who was unsettled as to her vocation. She was left alone in the world by the death of both parents. On top of this, she suffered a broken engagement. Although highly talented, she was wasting her time in mere drifting.

A young man, the middle one of three boys in his family. The oldest boy was the parents' favorite. When he died, the youngest became the favorite because he resembled the oldest. The middle boy felt the disfavor of his parents very keenly. He attempted suicide.

This appears at first to be a series of extreme cases, but they are less extreme than they seem. The average congregation can furnish reasonably close duplicates to some of these at a moment's notice. A pastor can never be quite sure what is going on behind the gay faces of the adolescents who look up at him from the church pews and greet him with such a show of carelessness at the close of the service. Sometimes the gayest are covering up the most. And even those who are basically happy and well adjusted still need the friendly counsel of a pastor from time to time on lesser problems.

It is therefore essential that a minister equip himself with as thorough a book knowledge of adolescent psychology, the simpler insights of psychiatry, and the art of counseling with individuals as he can possibly obtain. It is a painful experience to be called upon for help and not be able to give it.

Beyond this, a minister's supreme task is to keep the way wide open between his young people and himself. If barriers arise, it cannot reasonably be expected that the young people will tear them down. The minister must tear them down and keep them down, so that he may go freely to his young people and they may come to him. To this end he will give attention not only to the adults but also to the young people in his pastoral visitation, for he is the pastor of adolescents no less than of their parents. Likewise, a certain amount of easy, natural fellowship in games and socials, as well as in the more serious gatherings of the youth of a church, is invaluable for opening the way. Young people feel differently toward a minister once they have talked with him, worked with him, played with him. But, above all, the minister's own bearing and manner must testify to all that he is approachable. Young people know, without knowing how they know, whether they dare talk with their minister or not. Something tells them beyond a doubt whether he will become sentimental over their difficulties, or horrified, or righteously indignant. If they suspect that he will act in any of these ways, they will stay as far from him as the east is from the west. But if they feel sure that he will understand, and will love the sinner even while he hates the sin, and will think more of what can be done in the future than of what has been done in the past, they will go to him with almost anything. A fine touchstone not only of a minister's efficiency in youth work but also of his own personality is the number of young people who come to him individually for counsel and help, and who receive him kindly when he goes to them.

An article several years ago in the *International Journal of Religious Education* had for its title "A Light in the Parsonage Window." Aside from the value of the article itself, the title is unforgettable. It gathers up into one phrase much that has been said in the preceding pages concerning a minister and his young people. It speaks of a light of welcome to young people in the window not of the church but of the parsonage. It seems to say that if the church is to stay close to youth and youth to the church, there must first be a light in the *parsonage* window. Let us keep that light burning!

VIII

DEVELOPING LAY WORKERS

A KEY-ELEMENT in ministerial strategy is the training of workers for service. A theological professor who served for some years in a pastorate was recently reminiscing upon his pastoral experience. "If I had those years to live over again," he said, "I should spend much more time than I did in the training of workers. Instead of spreading myself out thin in a multitude of contacts and activities, I should try to gather about me a little inner circle, and I should concentrate on them." This would seem to be a sound strategy. The minister, like all other men, is strictly limited in the amount of time and energy he can devote to his calling. He can be only one place at a time, and that for only a short while. He is neither omnipresent nor everlasting. Hence he can multiply his usefulness greatly by surrounding himself with a corps of faithful and competent laymen who will become, as it were, undershepherds of the flock.

There are many other ways of investing his time which seem at first glance to promise larger returns. There are huge meetings to be addressed, and worldwide movements to be supported, and high-sounding committees to be set up. In the face of such spectacular ways of doing the work of a minister, it seems somewhat of a pity to waste one's time on a few persons meeting unobtrusively for quiet fellowship and study. Yet there is the best possible Christian precedent for so doing. For, as is well known, this was the chief strategy employed by Jesus. When it became apparent to Him that His ministry could not last over many months or years, it would have been entirely natural for Him to exhaust every device for reaching people by the thousands. Instead—with a far greater wisdom —He chose the strategy of developing a few workers. Resolutely He turned His back on the crowds, and as the precious months ebbed slowly away He sat contentedly pouring out the great riches of His mind and heart into the lives of a few apostles-to-be. That was the first Christian workers' conference; the first workers' training class. A Roman captain riding by, or a Pharisee, would have valued it at about a thousandth part of its true significance.

In the modern congregation it still remains true that good workers are of paramount importance. Many of the difficulties which perplex pastor and people are reducible finally to the problem of an adequate personnel. Supply that, and the difficulties are solved. Without that they are virtually insoluble. Sound principles, therefore, of good churchmanship undergird the rapidly growing movement of training workers for service. And there is every evidence that ministers are becoming increasingly sensitive to their own responsibilities in this connection. When the International Council of Religious Education several years ago asked a number of ministers what religious-education activities they regarded as of chief importance, the one which headed the list was: "conduct a session of a training class for present or prospective church-school leaders."[1]

[1] Mayer, O., *The Religious Education Activities of Three Hundred Pastors*. The International Council of Religious Education, 1932, p. 23.

DEVELOPING LAY WORKERS

How Are Workers Developed?

Let us imagine a young man twenty years of age, engaged in teaching a class of Junior boys. At his present stage of development he is unable to lift his eyes from his quarterly and tell a story to his boys; he must read it word for word. He soon gets completely lost if he undertakes to use the discussion method. He cannot offer a free prayer. He does not understand Junior boys. He is shy and timid, and far from certainty in his own religious experience. Yet the pastor looking on sees some latent abilities in this young man, and secretly sets him aside for the church-school superintendency some day. In his mind's eye he sees a man poised, resourceful, rich in religious experience, proficient in the art of human fellowship, conversant with the best knowledge available concerning the church school, and skilled with all the arts essential to the performance of the superintendent's work. How does this young man progress from here to there?

Clearly, experience alone will not accomplish the desired transformation. Experience is a great teacher, provided the pupil is brilliant and no one is in a hurry. If this young man is left to himself—to teach his class Sunday after Sunday without reading a book, or visiting a teacher at work, or attending a conference, or talking over his work with some experienced worker —his growth in ability will be painfully slow. If he is satisfied with himself, he may not grow at all in ten years. If he is dissatisfied, he will have to blunder slowly into better ways of teaching.

Just as clearly, knowledge alone will not bring about the desired result. He might conceivably give up his class of boys, and settle down to devote all his time to the acquisition of knowledge about church-school work. He might read books without number, attend conferences galore, and secure enough training credits to be the pride of the countryside, but he would not thereby be made into a competent worker. One does not learn to swim by taking a correspondence course.

It appears, therefore, that a person grows in good workmanship by *closely interwoven experience and knowledge*. (This is, of course, the principle which Professor William Heard Kilpatrick has made memorable for so many of his students.) If our hypothetical young man can have a half-hour of strenuous teaching experience with his Junior boys, and then just as much knowledge out of books or through contact with more capable teachers as he can absorb at that moment, and then another try at his class in the light of his greater knowledge, and then another approach to the sources of knowledge—he will grow in ability. If he is to master the art of storytelling, it must be in accordance with this formula. If his religious experience is to widen and deepen, it must be in accordance with this formula. This is the central principle to be remembered in all attempts to develop workers. The attempts will be successful in the degree in which they abide by this principle.

The ways or devices which are open to a pastor interested in developing a corps of capable and devout lay-workers are many. If the most important of these are assembled in one place, they constitute a bird's-eye view of an adequate training program for a congregation. If, in addition, numerical values be assigned each item, they become a standard by which a congregation may measure itself in this regard.

DEVELOPING LAY WORKERS

Standard for a Workers' Training Program in the Local Congregation

I. General Provisions for Workers' Training   150

1. Is some person made definitely responsible for recruiting and training workers in the congregation?   10

2. Is a careful canvass made each year of young people (as well as older) who show promise of ability but are not now active?   5

3. Is there an assistant-teacher plan whereby young people learn to be teachers or officers through apprenticeship?   15

4. Is adequate opportunity given young people in class, department, or society to conduct their own affairs under guidance?   10

5. Are all workers given a democratic share in considering and determining policies and plans of the church?   20

6. Does a sense of mission, the consciousness of a great and sacred task to be accomplished, pervade the church and its membership?   25

7. Is the congregation properly appreciative of the efforts of its lay workers?   5

8. Is there an annual public installation and consecration of officers and teachers?   5

9. Is there a workers' library, with some new books added each year and with a definite plan of reading for the workers?   10

10. Is there a plan whereby the workers receive regularly a good magazine on Christian education?   5

11. Does each worker read at least one Christian education journal regularly and at least one book on Christian education each year?   5

12. Is there a plan whereby each worker makes a worth-while visit to another church twice a year?   5

13. Do the workers consciously set goals for themselves through the annual use of teacher-standards or teacher rating-scales? 5

14. Is the work of the church of such high caliber that both present workers and the children and young people as well are learning the best methods through actual experience? (Standard B is the guide in answering this question so far as the church school is concerned.) 20

15. Are courses on the history and the present program of the church offered young people in church school, young people's society, or church-membership class? 5

II. Workers' Conferences 120

1. Does the school have a workers' conference approximately ten times a year? 15
2. Do all the workers attend these conferences? 10
3. Is an educational topic provided as the main feature of the workers' conference? 15
4. Is this topic, as a rule, concrete and specific? 10
5. Does the program provide for participation by the workers? 10
6. Are these programs planned as carefully as a session of a training class? 10
7. Do the conferences as a rule end in some definite plan of action? 5
8. Are the substitute or apprentice teachers participants in the conferences? 5
9. Do members of the official board meet at least four times a year in conference on topics relating to their work? 20
10. Are these programs planned and conducted as carefully as a session of a training class? 20

III. Supervision 9

1. Is some person made definitely responsible for supervising? 15

2. Does each worker have the benefit of two supervisory visits and conferences a year?   20

3. Would the supervisor's training and experience in Christian education qualify him to be an accredited instructor in the Standard Training Curriculum?   20

4. Is his personality and high Christian purpose such as to make his visits and guidance welcome to the leaders?   15

5. Do the conferences deal with such specific matters as: the needs of the persons under the worker's care, the methods employed, the materials employed, the worker's religious beliefs, etc.?   15

6. Is the supervisory plan running without undue friction?   5

IV. Training Classes and Schools   *80*

1. Does the church conduct or co-operate in conducting at least one Standard Training Class or School each year?   15

2. Is a syllabus constructed for each course which builds primarily upon the problems and interests of the class members and only secondarily on the text?   20

3. Is discussion amply provided for?   10

4. Is actual practice amply provided for before, during, and after the course?   10

5. Does the number of credits earned annually in this fashion plus those earned in summer camps and schools equal one half of the number of active workers in the church?   15

6. Are these credits earned chiefly by persons who now are or soon will be active workers in the church?   10

V. Co-operation with Regional or Denominational Agencies   *60*

1. Are one to six persons—depending on the size

195

and the financial ability of the church—sent to training camp or summer school each year?   20

2. Are these delegates carefully chosen?   10

3. Is the camp or school of sufficiently high educational level to have its courses accredited by the International Council of Religious Education?   10

4. Does the church send official delegates to at least two conventions or institutes each year?   10

5. Are these delegates carefully chosen for their ability to profit by the convention and to embody suggestions made there in the life of the church?   5

6. Do the conventions or institutes devote the major part of their sessions to thinking through several educational problems which are real to the delegates?   5

    ———

    500

If a congregation were to work consistently and conscientiously along all of these several lines for a period of ten years, checking and rechecking periodically to see if any important ones were being overlooked, it is safe to say that it would find itself in possession of a corps of lay workers who would make its work a joy during the succeeding ten years. It now remains to examine these several ways a bit more closely.

The Workers' Conference

There is nothing sacrosanct about the numerical weighting given the several items in the foregoing standard. Good reasons could be given for shifting the weightings up or down at a number of points.

However, in the judgment of many the workers' conference richly deserves the high place of importance given it in this standard. It has a function to perform in the training of workers for service which no other agency can fulfill.

For the workers' conference is nothing more or less than the life and task of a congregation come to consciousness. It is a device for lifting high a church's work bit by bit and getting it examined and made over in a setting of friendly fellowship. As such, naturalness is of the very essence of it. It dare not be regimented according to some preconceived pattern. A young minister went into his first congregation eager to hold a series of workers' conferences. He called the workers together, and announced a whole series of topics. They were good topics, as topics go, and the workers waded through them patiently, but the result could not be called workers' conferences. It is fatal to lay out a long series of topics. The topics must emerge month by month, and simply cry out for attention. It is equally fatal to invite a succession of speakers to appear before the workers. There is a place for speeches in the workers' conference, but only when the thought of the group has reached a point where a speech is needed to enable them to move on. Then let the speaker appear, provided he is given full instructions as to how he fits in. It is almost equally fatal to study a book chapter by chapter in the workers' conference, unless the workers themselves recognize that a certain book will enable them to move on from where they are to where they want to be.

The workers' conference, then, is a clear example of unbridled individualism. It can never be exactly the same in any two churches. In some it includes only the staff of the church school; in others it reaches out to take in workers in other auxiliaries as well. In some it meets monthly; in others, quarterly; in still others it meets weekly for a month or so and then desists for a while. In some it is a supper meeting; in others, not. In some it includes all the workers of a school; in others—particularly large churches—it divides into departmental groups. The chief rule it must follow is "Be natural."

There is, likewise, a great variety in type of program. Some church schools make it a practice to begin with a business session, and then move over into the conference proper. If this is done, care must be taken to close the business session at a prearranged time. Nothing will kill a conference more quickly than long-drawn-out discussions of business minutiae which a small committee could handle much better than the entire group of workers. Some conferences make a point of including each time a living, breathing report by departmental principals or heads of organizations before moving on to the major topic for the evening. Others include each time a preliminary "Problem Period" in which each worker is free to bring before the whole group some problem which is resting heavily upon him. A growing number of schools are adopting the practice of devoting the conference in the month before each new quarter to a "preview" of the materials for the coming quarter and an earnest discussion of how to make the best use of them.

It may be helpful to include several actual instances of conferences or conference plans. As an illustration at once of a somewhat more formal program for a conference and also of one way of launching conferences in a church where they have never been held, we may look at the following procedure. First of all, the chart below is reproduced on a blackboard.

OUR CHURCH'S OBJECTIVES THIS COMING YEAR

	Three of general importance	Needs of individuals	Welfare of community	Emphasis Jesus would desire	Three that have been stressed
1. To make God real to our members, young and old.					
2. To train them in worship.					
3. To make the teachings of Jesus real to them.					
4. To develop in them a personal loyalty to Jesus.					
5. To help them think through their personal problems.					
6. To help them think through social problems.					
7. To develop in them a real sympathy with others.					
8. To give them a chance to live with a group in fellowship.					
9. To make them workers for a Christian social order.					
10. To teach them the story of the Christian Church.					
11. To develop in them a loyalty to the church.					
12. To give them a Christian attitude toward trouble.					
13. To teach them the facts of the Bible.					
14. To bring them to love the Bible.					

The purpose of this conference is to set a group thinking seriously and yet interestingly on the objectives of their work. It will be recognized that these objectives are an adaptation of the seven developed by Dr. Paul H. Vieth. The plan as outlined here has actually been used to good effect in several churches.

After sufficient time is spent on each of the fourteen objectives to get the group of workers thinking about them in terms of their own classes or organizations, the leader says: "If you had to select three of these, and only three, to be stressed by this church during the coming year, which three would they be?" The vote is taken, recorded in the first column, noted by a secretary, and then erased from the board. The leader then says: "Now think only of the needs of the persons for whom you are responsible. If you had to select the three most important to the unfolding of their lives, which three would they be?" Again the vote is taken, recorded in the second column, noted in the secretary's record, and erased from the board. For the third column the question is: "Now think only of the good of our community. Which three would you now select?" A similar procedure is followed. For the fourth column the question is: "Now put out of your minds everything except Jesus, His life and His teachings. Which three would He have us stress?" For the fifth column the query is: "Which three have we stressed during the past several years?" At the end, the figures are all re-entered in the five columns from the secretary's notes, and comparisons are in order. By this time, it is generally difficult to hold the group of workers in check. At many points in those five columns striking implications stand out not only for the work of the church but also for future conferences.

As an illustration of a conference plan which on the basis of rather careful preparation attempts to get down to rock-bottom at one sector of a church-school's life, the following is instructive. It was prepared by a theological student, who was at the time supplying a small congregation.

Attendance

Specific problem to be faced: Church-school attendance on the Sundays when there is no church service.

Advance assignment: Each teacher to study the attendance record of the members of his class for the past year. Officers to study the records of the divisions and the school as a whole for the past year. Reasons for absences to be noted in so far as possible.

Opening devotions: In charge of the workers of the children's division.

Talk: The importance of regular attendance, by the superintendent.

Report of secretary: What the records show.

Reports of teachers: Percentages of attendance in each class, etc.

Discussion on basis of reports: Where the largest number of absences occur, when, what particular pupils, reasons, etc.

Report of secretary: Showing the attendance record of the workers for the past year. Comparison with the pupils' records. Possible connection between the two. Effect of teacher's absence on pupil. Effect on teaching work. Effect on teacher.

What can we do about it?

Possibility of increasing our own regularity of attendance.

Possible improvements in the church-school hour to attract pupils.

Worship service—pupil participation, variety, richness.

Teaching of the lesson—pupil participation, connection with life, more adequate preparation, outside materials.

Selection of materials—based on pupil interests, from more sources.

Follow-up of absentees.

What we do now when a pupil is absent (usually very little).

What effect does this have upon the pupil?

What should we do? Cultivate practice of telephoning or calling during the next week by either the teacher or the class members.

Class emphasis upon attendance at appropriate times.

School recognition of attendance—Rally Day, perfect-attendance classes each Sunday.

What shall we do about it?

Discussions possibly crystallizing in a pledge of regular attendance unless positively prevented from coming, of taking more active account of absences of pupils, of striving to make best attendance record during the coming year.

Closing devotions.

Adjournment.

Such is the workers' conference. It is the power-house of the modern church. It is the present-day equivalent of the prayer meeting. Fortunately, it stands a good chance of generating light as well as heat.

SUPERVISION

This is a thoroughly objectionable word for a thoroughly worth-while way of training workers. The word has been traveling in bad company for so long that it has become corrupted. It carries now the connotations of "over" and "under," of spying and checking up, of arbitrary directions given by one who knows to one who does not know. The chances are that it ought never to be allowed to escape from the pages of a book. It has a certain usefulness there, but scarcely ever in conversation between a minister and his lay workers.

What we have in mind, of course, is two friends— the one perhaps more experienced and the other less —considering together some item in the work of a church with which both are familiar. The one is familiar with it because he has been responsible for it all along—the teaching of a class, or the leading of a worship service, or the planning of a program for a young people's society. The other has made himself familiar with it by visitation in order that he might be of maximum help. No one can hit off better the essential idea of Christian supervision than Doctor Coe, when he says: "The fundamental idea in supervision is intimate sharing in burden-bearing." That is what it is! It is two people carrying a responsibility together, whereas before there was only one.

Supervision, thus interpreted, can do something toward improving a church's program as well as improving a church's workers that no other method can quite duplicate. It brings help to the earnest, groping, ofttimes disheartened servant of the church at the time he most needs it, at the points where he most needs it, and in the way that will help him most. It is the example par excellence of knowledge being geared directly into experience. Hard as it is to accomplish, it is a question whether a church can afford to get along without it. The public-school system would never attempt for a moment to get along without it. A large part of a young person's training in the modern teachers' college consists of practice teaching under the skilled yet kindly eye of a supervisor, who helps him diagnose his own ills and apply his own remedies. And after he is appointed to his first position, the quality of his work and his own professional advancement are safeguarded by continued supervision. And—to return once more to the church and its work—there is every evidence that we are paying a heavy price for attempting to get along without supervision. A minister in charge of a vacation school was prevented during the first half of the school from doing any supervising. When he finally shook himself loose from his manifold duties and began to do what he should have done from the beginning, he found that one or two key classes in the Junior Department were getting exactly nowhere. The teachers of these classes had reported no difficulties in the teachers' conferences. In no other way than through supervision could these difficulties have been brought to light and corrected.

Who shall do this work of supervision in the average church? Often there is a capable public-school teacher with additional training and experience in Christian education who can assume this responsibility for the children's work of the church. Her competence, of course, must be beyond question and her personality well on the way to the angelic, else she is defeated before she starts. Fortunately, there are such persons! In many churches, part, at least, of the supervising must be done by the pastor if it is to be done at all. Teachers will frequently seek and accept help from him more readily than they would from one of their own number. Only he must have prepared himself by study and by actual experience with childhood and youth to render this help, or he will forfeit their confidence. Can a busy pastor take the time for supervision? The answer is that he can—and he will, if it is sufficiently worth while.

How shall supervision be introduced in a congregation where it is unknown? Obviously, it is not the sort of thing to be launched with a grand flourish of announcements. The minister can, if he desires, talk it over in the quiet fellowship of a workers' conference. He can make clear that he has no intentions of "dropping in" unannounced on unsuspecting teachers; that he renounces all claims to omniscience in the teaching of a class or the conduct of a worship service; that he would hope to take one department at a time and work with its teachers until they and he felt that definite strides were being made. The workers may receive such a plan enthusiastically—and again they may not! A better plan—far better—is for supervision to grow up naturally and, if possible, at the request of the workers themselves. For example, a certain minister had met with the teachers of his Primary Department in group conference. This conference had a sequel in the case of Miss X. He describes it as follows:

On October 25 this teacher, Miss X, came to the parsonage. She had told me she was coming in, and I did my best to anticipate her coming by making certain preparations. When she arrived, she told me she came to inform me that the work of this class was too difficult for her, and that therefore she wanted to give up her work. I expected this. We talked the matter over for some time. A few questions revealed the fact that she did not know how to use her teacher's manual. Also a question of discipline had proved troublesome the Sunday before. Then we came to the teaching of the lesson. We turned to the lesson for the coming Sunday. I pointed out to her what I should seek to accomplish in teaching that lesson if I were the teacher; how I should begin, the very words I should use; and how I should go through this particular lesson step by step, with each step growing out of what went before. She told me she had difficulty in telling the lesson story and had to read part of it, thereby losing the attention of her pupils. I suggested that she outline the story, and with her I outlined the story of the lesson we were studying. I told her to type the outline, and take it with her to the class. This conference seemed to encourage her. She seemed to begin to see how the different parts of the lesson hung together. Then I gave her a book to read, parts of which I had marked before she came. I went over this with her and asked her to take it home and read it. Nothing since has been said about giving up her class. I gave her a series of lesson plans for December, and a series for January.

This is not a perfect example of supervision, as the minister in question would be the first to admit. Too much was done for Miss X, and not enough with her. Nevertheless, it served to give her a fresh start in her teaching, and it illustrates the best possible way for supervision to get started in a congregation.

One more instance of supervision may be in order. This too is not a perfect instance. It does exemplify, however, some of the items to be noted in visiting a class, and it embodies some sound principles of procedure in the supervisory conference. The class which was being taught was an adult class made up entirely of people in middle life and over. The supervisor was a young man not yet in the ministry. This was his first experience of this sort. He describes it rather whimsically as follows:

THE SUPERVISORY VISIT

1. Physical conditions:

Lighting and ventilation satisfactory.

Routine: Songs, responsive Scripture, reading of lesson (from the Bible), prayer for pardon, general prayer by pastor, etc., with other classes. Study period with no interference from other classes. Closing song and Lord's Prayer with other classes.

Materials: International S. S. Quarterly à la Heidelberg Press.

2. Personal factors in leader:

Neat appearance; good voice; no distracting mannerisms; acceptable language; accepts Bible literally.

3. *The class's program as a whole:*

> Meets regularly every Sunday morning.
>
> Class meetings at homes of the members once per month (with abundant refreshments).
>
> Celebrates anniversary of the organized class each year at a special Sunday-evening service.
>
> Co-operates with church suppers, etc.

4. *This particular session:*

> Topic: "Becoming a Christian." Acts 16. 22-34; Phil. 3. 7-14.
>
> Apparent aim: To cover the printed portion of Scripture, and enlarge upon it.
>
> Apparent results: The class members felt that the lesson had been covered.
>
> General interest: Class members were quiet and attentive after the collection had been taken. (The taking of the collection was very noisy.)

5. *Class procedure in some detail:*

> Opened with prayer, during which there was quiet and reverence. Then both the teacher and the secretary began their labors. The taking of the collection was unusually noisy. But once the coins were safely placed in an envelope, all became quiet and the class members were attentive.
>
> Becoming a Christian was compared with and made equivalent to becoming a church member. It was made clear, both seriously and humorously, that there is no good excuse for not becoming a church member.
>
> Following this brief introduction, each verse of the printed Scripture lesson was taken separately and enlarged upon. Modern applications were inserted throughout.
>
> It was insisted upon that the earthquake was an act of intervention on the part of God in response to the prayers and songs of Paul and Silas. (It is possible that this particular appeared magnified to me because of my disagreement.)
>
> Apparently no conclusion.

THE SUPERVISORY CONFERENCE

The teacher said that he had no particular aim in mind, but on second thought said that he could say his aim was to show the advantages of being a Christian. It appeared from the conversation that the only advantage of being a Christian was that it made one happy. "Christianity made the jail-keeper happy." "It made the seller of purple happy."

He thought that he answered the question of what it means to become a Christian in the illustration of the experience of the jail-keeper. However, to the best of my memory, he did not enlarge upon the formula, "Believe on the Lord Jesus Christ." The verse was simply quoted as being the answer.

I inquired as to whether he thought it might have been more effective simply to enlarge upon the above-mentioned answer, rather than try to cover so much territory. He didn't think that it would have been, for people of that age. Whereupon, I hinted at the possibility of minimizing the majority of the verses and making clear the meaning of the one outstanding verse.

The victim of my inquiry remarked that he supposed his method was what Professor ————— called the lazy way of teaching. (He said that it was the method used by the pastor of the church during the first few Sundays observed before he began to teach. I hereby wash my hands of the report.)

The matter of the noisy collection will be brought up at the meeting of the class. The teacher will inquire whether he should wait until the offering is taken before beginning his discourse. (Of the results I know not.)

In what was given the color of an extra-conference discussion we talked about the matter of prayer. He is open-minded. Also he is in a state of confusion. The things taught in the seminary seem correct, but they are different from his former ideas. (I did not attempt to impregnate him with heterodoxy.)

I felt a bit uncomfortable about the whole matter at first, fearing that perhaps he would feel that I, not much further advanced than he, was sitting in judgment of him. Much of this feeling was, I believe, offset by the fact that we have at least one factor in common in our backgrounds—both attended the same college. This fact made the conference much easier, I know. Perhaps having at least one interest in common with the teacher, other than the class, is the key—or one of the keys—to supervision. At any rate, we are still friends in spite of this experiment in supervision.

THE WORKERS' TRAINING CLASS

Like each of the other agencies for developing workers, this one has its own distinctive place which nothing else can fill. It lends itself especially to the systematic covering of some area of study. The new training curriculum projected by some forty major denominations through the International Council of Religious Education is an instrument of marvelous flexibility. It provides courses on four levels of difficulty and on almost every imaginable subject profitable for enriching the worker's own life or heightening his value to his church. There are courses which the person who lacks even a high-school diploma can tackle without fear, and courses to challenge the intellect of the college graduate. There are courses on the Bible, Christian doctrine, psychology, teaching method, worship, and how to set up a co-operative. There are courses for Kindergarten teachers, for musicians, and for members of the official board. It is a heartening picture to conjure up before the mind's eye of classes of earnest people from coast to coast studying to show themselves approved unto God, workmen who need not be ashamed.

In many places the conduct of training classes can best be done on a community-wide basis. It is properly a task for an entire community. For one thing, the source of supply of teachers is thereby greatly widened; for another, the inspiration which comes from seeing the church workers of a community gathered together in one place for training is not to be despised. It is impossible here, however, to discuss the practical issues which arise in setting up and maintaining a Community Training School. The bulletins of the International Council of Religious Education attend to that well. We must here confine ourselves primarily to the situation which a pastor confronts in setting up his own class in his own church. As a matter of fact, some pastors desire classes of their own occasionally even while supporting to the full a community school. Then, too, there is often no community school.

The growth of a training class can never be forced. It must come about naturally. For this reason a very large class at the outset is generally unhealthy. One young minister, desiring to start a class, canvassed personally the potential students in the congregation and succeeded in beginning with an enrollment of forty. He was much elated at first, but found to his great disappointment that the numbers dwindled almost as rapidly as Gideon's band. Far healthier was the beginning made by another minister—or, rather, by the teachers themselves, for it was they who took the initiative. A workers' conference had been held which gave rise to a discussion of the use of the Bible in the department. The minister writes:

Out of this meeting came a discussion of the use of the Bible in the department. This culminated in the acknowledgment on the part of the teachers that they did not know enough about the Bible. Several expressed the desire for information. The next day one of the teachers called my wife and told her that she felt the need for

information about the Bible, and that she would be interested in a teacher-training class.

This led to the circulation on the following Sunday
among the teachers of a list of the problems which might
be discussed in a leadership-training class with the New
Testament as the subject. Twelve to fifteen favorable
responses came from teachers and others as a result of the
circulation of this paper. Consequently, the work of this
class in Course 4 (old numbering) of the Standard Leadership Training Curriculum had its beginning last
Wednesday evening with sixteen students present.

Once the initial move is well and wisely made, the
class's success will depend largely on the teacher's skill
in keeping the movement of the course close to the
students themselves. It must be their class, first, last,
and always, and they must feel it to be such. The outline of the course must be built upon the student's
own problems and interests. This is much easier to
do in a course on teaching method or on psychology,
but even in a course on the Bible the students' own
individual perplexities about the Bible can be allowed
to rise to the surface in every session. The course will
mean much more to the students if every last one of
them carries some definite responsibility in the church,
even though it be only for the duration of the course.
Then their several experiences in class or worship
service or the home or the community must be allowed
to run in and out constantly through all the class sessions. Indeed, it is these very experiences which ought
to form the warp and woof of the fabric of the class.

The meaning of the foregoing sentences is an open
book to an old and experienced teacher. To one who
has had little teaching experience they may carry no
concrete suggestions. We may, therefore, examine
with profit an actual course-plan which was utilized in

a large class of about fifty students with good results. It was designed by a minister's wife, but it is nothing new for ministers to learn from ministers' wives. The course in question is No. 210b, entitled "The Growth of Christian Personality During Childhood." It is therefore a course in child psychology, with particular emphasis upon the religious growth of children. The members of the class were chiefly teachers of children —women for the most part. The course-plan is worked out on the regulation form supplied by the International Council of Religious Education. Omitting the introductory section which deals with matters irrelevant in this connection, the plan continues as follows:

II. *What is your aim for this course? When you answer this question regarding your aim, you might have in mind such questions as the following: In what attitudes do you hope your students will improve? What new knowledge do you hope they will gain? In what skills do you wish them to make improvement? Please be as specific as possible so that you can show where you think the central emphasis of the course should be placed. Your explanation should be so specific that it could not apply to any other course in the leadership curriculum.*

1. To help leaders of children to feel that their task is one of guiding children in growth of Christian personality in conscious co-operation with the purposes of God.

2. To lead them to understand the fundamentals of behavior—attitudes, ideas, habits, skills.

3. To lead them to discover specific opportunities in which they as leaders may change that behavior which is negative to the development of Christian personality, and strengthen that behavior which is positive.

III. *What major topics or questions do you now think your students should deal with in this course? This list, or outline, can well be the basis for your more detailed preparation. All major topics or questions essential to a consideration of the field of this course should be included, with enough minor questions to make the major topics clear. (It is understood that you may change these questions somewhat when you become better acquainted with the specific needs of your students.) Each question will have, of course, a direct relationship to the aim, and will be within the field of the course.*

1. What is your conception of your task as a teacher of religion?

   What is Christian personality?

2. What are the laws of growth?

   How do the native endowments and characteristics of children at different age levels affect our materials and objectives in religious education?

3. What is the effect of environment on the development of Christian personality?

   Social and economic situations of the family? Contacts with other races and nationalities? Physical condition and nurture? Children in the home? Companions?

4. What are the normal and abnormal behavior problems of children at different age levels?

   Fear, obedience, insecurity, inferiority, aggressiveness, sex, honesty, nervousness, mental deficiency, shyness, etc.

   What are the underlying causes or stimuli which have produced these reactions?

   What attitudes and procedures of leaders help children to meet these problems and to discover Christian solutions to them?

5. How do a child's purposes and ideals for himself grow?

   How does participation of the child, to the extent of his ability, in the building of a Christian society make for growth of Christian personality?

6. How are ideas formed? How do attitudes develop? How are habits built?

   How can a leader help a child to change an attitude? to develop a new habit?

7. What are the religious ideas and needs of children at different age levels?

    What ideas of God do we wish our children to form?

    How do their ideas of God develop?

    How may a growing sense of companionship with Jesus influence the child's development?

IV. *What assignments do you now have in mind that you think are suitable for this course? You may wish to use some of the assignments in the leader's guide. In addition, it seems desirable to have some that grow out of your own planning for the course. Please describe as exactly and fully as you can, in the space allowed, several such assignments.*

1. Select an undesirable attitude or habit present in a member of your class or in the entire class. Outline your procedure in trying to change that attitude or habit to one that is Christian.

2. Evaluate your church-school objectives, materials, and procedures for a particular department. Are they consistent with the child's interests, capacities, and skills? In the light of this study, can you suggest any improvements?

3. Discover what are the common fears of a group of children at a specific age level. Discover, if possible, what underlying causes have brought about these reactions. Suggest a possible means of overcoming the fears.

4. List the unchristian or superstitious ideas of God prevalent in children. Evaluate your own teaching and materials to discover whether you have unconsciously helped to foster any of these misconceptions.

5. Make a case study of a particular child. List his normal capacities, interests, and skills. List any abnormalities, or behavior problems. Note the effect of his particular environment upon his personality development. Suggest any help which a church-school leader could give to this child to foster the development of his Christian personality.

V. *What teaching procedures will you use? (Although the space is limited you can give considerable information if you use a short phrase rather than a complete sentence for each idea.)*

    1. *If you plan to try to discover the interests and needs of your students, how will this be done in the first and later sessions?*

Each student will check his three preferences on a prepared list of problems covering the scope of the course. Course will be built around these selected interests. I will be alert to needs of students which will show themselves during later discussion.

    2. *Do you plan that the students shall share in the decisions regarding what shall be done in the course during class sessions and outside of class sessions?*

Yes.

    If so, what opportunities will there be for them to do so in the first session and in later sessions?

First session—use of problem list mentioned above. Students submit any additional problems. Class decide whether or not in scope of course.

Students given choice in matter of assignments.

    3. *Exactly how will the work which the students do on assignments be related to what is done during the class sessions?*

Class divided into committees for assignments according to their interests, using problem sheet as basis. Each committee make report to class, followed by class discussion.

    4. *The foregoing questions emphasize the students' share in the teaching-learning enterprise. What specific contributions shall you as instructor try to make to the class?*

Resource leader. Refer class to suitable source materials.

Guide discussions, so that correct and helpful conclusions may be reached.

Supplement class discussions and reports by the presentation of helpful material.

5. *What major teaching methods shall you use and about what proportion of the total class time of the course will be given to each?*
Discussion—50 per cent.
Assigned reports—25 per cent.
Leader's presentations—25 per cent.

. . . . . .

In conclusion, it must be recognized that an adequate program of training workers for service is not to be achieved by adding one device to another in mathematical fashion. A congregation might conceivably have all of these developed to mechanical perfection, and find Saint Paul saying to it as he said to the Christians at Corinth, "yet show I unto you a more excellent way." The primary requisite for a congregation that would develop its lay personnel is to be engaged in doing something that it knows to be genuinely worth while and to give as many people as possible a real share in the doing of it. In the final analysis, a competent corps of workers comes to a congregation as a by-product of a co-operative quest for the kingdom of God.

IX

REACHING THE HOME

It is not often that class-discussions are remembered vividly ten or fifteen years after they took place. About that long ago there was, however, such a discussion in one of the major theological seminaries of our country. A brilliant young instructor was in the chair. He submitted to a startled class the thesis that perhaps it might be just as well for the church to abandon all its efforts to call people within its walls and influence them there. Since the home was the place where real personality-development was taking place daily and hourly, why not concentrate our efforts there? Let the church, therefore, become a mere office building —a place where a number of home-consultants would have their headquarters. There might be a person specially trained in religion; another in psychology; another in medicine; yet another in homecraft; and so on. These advisers would ply back and forth between the central church and the homes of the congregation, bearing help and guidance of the sort required at the time when it was needed most. In this way the church would become a true minister to an institution far older than the church and perhaps far more important—the home.

Now, of course, this thesis in its extreme form is on the face of it false, as both professor and students knew full well. Yet, if anyone wanted to defend such a proposal, he could assemble an imposing array of arguments in its support—arguments which at the very least prove that the home merits the serious attention of the church.

WHY SO MUCH CONCERN ABOUT THE HOME?

The answer to this question may best be given in a series of statements, each of which can be supported not only by everyday observation but also by cold, undebatable statistics.

To begin with, *the home has a profound influence on the character of individuals.* Some years ago the Character Education Inquiry was engaged in the most laborious study of human nature which this planet has seen. Among other things, the investigators measured the knowledge of right and wrong possessed by hundreds of children. They were curious to know how much resemblance there was between these children's judgments and the judgments of those with whom they were in daily contact. Their findings are a tribute to the moral potency of the home, for the mothers and fathers stood head and shoulders above all other persons who might influence these children in their notions of right and wrong (the coefficient of correlation was found to be .545). Incidentally, the mothers were far ahead of the fathers in this regard. Next came the children's friends, with a correlation of .353. Next their club leaders (.137)! Next their public-school teachers (.028)! And almost at the vanishing point of influence were their church-school teachers (.002)![1] But it is possible to go farther and cite statistics which concern not mere moral knowledge but actual conduct. During recent years the

---

[1] *Religious Education,* 1926, pp. 539ff. "Testing the Knowledge of Right and Wrong," by H. Hartshorne, M. A. May, D. E. Sonquist, and C. A. Kerr.

county of Los Angeles has become aroused over the wave of delinquency with which it has had to contend. In the effort to understand and cope with this problem, it has made careful case-studies of 14,000 delinquents. The facts are that 37 per cent of the boy delinquents and 54 per cent of the girls came from homes broken by death, divorce, or separation.[2]

Again, *the home has a profound influence on the personality make-up of individuals.* It not only shapes their moral knowledge and conduct for either good or ill, but reaches to the very depths of their personalities to determine largely whether they shall be happy or unhappy, timid or bold, buoyant or depressed. In preparation for the recent White House Conference on Child Health and Protection, one of the committees set out to find fifty children who were adjudged happy by all who had dealings with them and fifty more who were just as unanimously accounted unhappy. Having found the children, it asked the eternal question, Why? What made the one set happy? And the other set unhappy? A number of possible causes were investigated carefully, but the inquiry seemed predetermined to come out where we might expect it would. In almost every instance it proved to be a case of a happy home versus an unhappy one.[3]

Again, *the home has a profound influence upon the religious interest of individuals.* If some men and women of a community are actively interested in religion, while others seem hopelessly indifferent, one reason is likely to be the homes of their childhood. An investigator made a study of a number of adults

---

[2] Scudder, K. J., and Beam, K. S., *Who Is Delinquent?* Rotary Club of Los Angeles, California, 1934, p. 9.

[3] Reported in *The Church and the Children*, by M. A. Jones. Cokesbury Press, 1935, pp. 241-2.

who showed widely varying degrees of interest in religious things, ranging all the way from theological students to out-and-out atheists. Was there any way of accounting for this wide divergence? Once more the trail ran back to the home! Did these people attend church school in their childhood? Were their mothers deeply religious? And their fathers? Was family worship practiced in their homes? Did their parents attend church? It was found—as we might expect—that people who stood high in as many as four of these home influences were four times as likely when they were grown to be given consistently to prayer as to be counted among those who never prayed. Similarly, those who ranked high in as many as four of these influences were five times as likely in their adulthood to be ministers of the church as to be outside the church altogether.[4]

Once more, *the home has a profound influence upon the attendance of individuals at the services of the church and its auxiliaries.* There was once a church school which, like many others, was distressed over the irregular attendance of its pupils; but, unlike many others, it set out to find the reasons and the remedies. Accordingly, it undertook to subject every single absence to a microscopic study. This it did over a six months' period, and with all the pupils under the adult division. It was found that the causes for the absences could be grouped conveniently into two large classes. On the one hand were certain causes centering in the school itself—classes without teachers, inadequate equipment, and the like. On the other hand were a

[4] Woodward, L. E., *Relations of Religious Training and Life Patterns to the Adult Religious Life.* Bureau of Publications, Teachers College, Columbia University, 1932, pp. 41-2.

number of causes centering in the home—indifference of parents, week-end trips, illness, and the like. The revelation came when a count was made of the two groups. In the Beginners Department 93 per cent of the reasons for absences were found to be in the home group. Even in the Senior High Department, where pupils are supposed to be very critical of the church school and very independent of home influence, 50 per cent of the reasons still remained in this group.[5]

And, finally, *the home has a profound influence upon the home life of the next generation.* At no point in life is it truer than here that the sins of the fathers are visited upon the children even to the third and fourth generations. A single case from the literature of psychology may serve to illuminate the point in question.[6] The account begins with a little boy who was an only child. When he was six, his father died, leaving the boy and his mother to share the life of the home. It would be only natural that an unusually close attachment should grow up between these two— an attachment whose effects were to be seen two generations later. In the course of time the boy became a man, and married. The life of the new home was fairly happy for a while, although the husband was moody by spells, and at times strangely indifferent toward his wife. The first child of this marriage was a boy, of whom the father soon became jealous. The second child was a little girl. Here at last was someone to love. Here was an outlet for the pent-up immature emotions of the father. And so his affections turned toward his little daughter. The outcome of it all was

[5] *International Journal of Religious Education,* July, 1930, pp. 27f. "Why Pupils Miss Sunday School," by O. M. Walton.

[6] Pierce, F., *Understanding Our Children.* E. P. Dutton and Co., Inc., 1925, pp. 4-10.

a disastrous alignment within this home—father and daughter against mother and son. At the time this case-study was written the boy and girl were apparently approaching adolescence. The tension between the parents had not lessened. The son was throwing in his lot with a set of companions who could do him little good and much harm. The daughter was living more and more in an imaginary world—a world of daydreaming and books. The son and daughter will in time probably marry, and have sons and daughters of their own. What will be the effect on them? And will the train of consequences never end? If it is to end this side of the Judgment Day, somebody or some institution must step in with wise counsel concerning the realities of home life.

It does look, then, as though more than a fair share of the determinants of life are lodged in the home. And it becomes transparently clear why any church that really wants to accomplish that whereunto it feels itself commissioned dare not ignore the homes in which its people live. For these homes, dotting the community, may truly be regarded as branch offices wherein much of the real business of the Kingdom is transacted. It would be folly to ignore these branches through an unwise preoccupation with the affairs of the central office.

But the picture is not yet complete! *In our day this all-important institution appears to have fallen upon evil times.* It is beset by unusual difficulties, under the stress of which it threatens to fall slowly apart. The most notorious evidence of this disintegration is the steadily mounting divorce rate. A conservative estimate would have it that of every six marriages today in the United States one is destined to end in the divorce court.[7]   But divorce is merely one indication of a general weakening of family ties.

About ten years ago the Lynds gave us a vivid picture of the changes which were taking place in the homes of the typical Midwestern city which they studied.   They wrote of a shrinkage in the very size of the plots of ground on which the homes were built.[8]   From the 1880's to the time of writing the frontage of the average lot in Middletown had decreased from 62½ feet to 40 feet.   Formerly there had been only eight lots to a block; now the real-estate men were squeezing in ten to fourteen.   Besides, the back of a lot was sometimes lopped off to make room for a house fronting on the alley.   Also, a slice was frequently taken from the side of a lot to provide a driveway to the garage. On the tiny spot of good earth which remained a house would be built.   But the house had fewer rooms than formerly.[9]   The parlor was fast becoming extinct, as was the spare bedroom.   And this shrinkage in space and size was merely a symbol of the fact that something else was also on the decline—namely, the amount of time the members of a family spent together and the number of interests which they held in common. Going to the local high school, the Lynds discovered that 55 per cent of the boys and 44 per cent of the girls were out of their homes four evenings or more a week on an average.[10]   A homely—yet rather pathetic —touch was furnished by the observation that in 1890 only about one fourth of the bread eaten in

---

[7] *Recent Social Trends.* McGraw-Hill Book Co., Inc., 1933. Vol. I, p. 693.

[8] Lynd, R. S., and Lynd, H. M., *Middletown.* Harcourt, Brace and Company, Inc., 1929, p. 94.

[9] *Ibid.*, pp. 98 and 99.

[10] *Ibid.*, p. 135.

Middletown came from bakeries; at the time of the study this proportion had risen to about two thirds.[11] And truly pathetic was the appointment of a Dean of Women in the local high school, because working-class mothers particularly had no time for talking heart-to-heart with their daughters.[12] These things were happening to home life in Middletown.

More recently, President Hoover's famous commission of social scientists have painted the same picture in even deeper colors. They tell us that in Chicago 45 per cent of all the apartments built during 1913-1917 had less than five rooms; by 1927-1931 this figure had risen to 75 per cent.[13] A home, like any other living thing, demands a certain amount of space; if denied that, it threatens to become weak and anemic. They tell us, further, that among 1,000 homes studied in 1930, two thirds of the farm houses even were dependent on baker's bread altogether.[14] Baking-day, for all its labors, used to be an event in the life of a home, and a tie by which parents and children were bound together. It is hard for fifteen cents on the window sill and a sign in the window to serve the same high purpose! And, as we might expect, the religious observances of family life are also finding it hard to maintain themselves. In an inquiry made in 1930 among school children, all of them white and American-born, it was found that only about one in eight came from a home that knew family worship.[15]

It seems, then, that the phrase "the centrifugal fam-

---

[11] *Ibid.*, p. 155.
[12] *Ibid.*, p. 134.
[13] *Recent Social Trends.* McGraw-Hill Book Co., Inc., 1933, Vol. I, p. 667.
[14] *Ibid.*, p. 664.
[15] *Ibid.*, p. 674.

ily" which Dr. George Walter Fiske used so effectively
is more than a figure of speech. Very gradually and
undramatically the American home is flying apart. Its
functions shake loose, one by one, and find lodgment
in some other institution in the community—a school
perhaps, or a playground, or a bakery. Its doors swing
open in the morning, and again in the evening after
supper, and the family—like that strange character in
the nonsense novel—mounts on horseback and rides
rapidly off in all directions.

This, then, together with the abiding importance of
the family for human well-being, accounts for the
present concern over the home. This is why major
denominations are thinking more and more seriously
about parental education. This is why the International Council of Religious Education selected as its
annual emphasis for a recent year "Christ in the Life
of the Home." This is why secular institutions, such
as the public school and the newer alphabetical agencies of government, are rushing to the home's support.
There is every reason why the local church too should
concern itself for the home.

There are many feasible ways by which a church
can reach its homes. Much can be done through wise
preaching which unites the age-old gospel with the
very new sciences of sociology and psychology to give
help to the members of homes. Excellent literature is
available (much of it in inexpensive pamphlet form),
whose wide distribution might bless many a home.
Mother's Day and Father's Day are opportunities wait-
ing to be given an educational turn. Very often the
crying need of the home is for something far more substantial than a bit of nicely applied psychology; it
needs first of all a chance to exist decently. It needs

a living wage, and proper working hours. It needs birth-control clinics. It needs sensible marriage laws. At all such points the church needs to come to the home's rescue.

In addition to the foregoing, there are several further ways which are largely undeveloped at present and promise rich returns to any minister who will enter upon them.

THE PARENTS' CLASS

The chief problem with regard to the parents' class is not at all what to do with the mothers and fathers after they arrive. There is a growing body of experience and literature which is quite helpful on the problems to be taken up, the procedures to be followed, and the like. The chief problem is how to get the parents there in the first place. More than one church has made hopeful plans for such a class, only to be met with an attendance so slight as to cast cold water on the project for months to come.

The most likely solution would seem to be along the line of capturing fathers and mothers for training in parenthood when they are already at the church—particularly during the church-school hour. There are many parents in the average church school, and very often there are whole classes made up entirely of the parents of small children. This looks like a golden opportunity, and it is. What a pity that it is so frequently lost on a mere study of the International Uniform Lessons! In a survey made recently of over two hundred young married people's groups in the churches of southern California, it was found that 71 per cent of these groups were content to use the Uniform Lessons.[16] What a waste of opportunity! Each adult class whose membership consists largely of parents might well devote at least one quarter of every year to a consideration of the Christian home.

For a variety of reasons, however, we cannot trust entirely to a proper use of the church-school hour. There are situations where a special class at some other time seems the best solution. How, then, shall parents be induced to come? A rather interesting strategy was employed by one church which had never had a parents' class during a history of over two hundred years. It was necessary, therefore, to start from scratch.

First of all, the matter was thoroughly discussed by the officers and teachers of the church school at one of their workers' conferences. Next it was laid before the official board of the church to receive their sanction. It was decided that the month of February should be given over to a home-emphasis with sermons appropriate to the theme, and that there should be a short-term parents' class with four weekly meetings—no more and no less. At this point—and here lies the key-element in the strategy—the promotion of the class was entrusted to a representative committee of parents. It was a good-sized committee, numbering fifteen or twenty fathers and mothers. It was this committee which went over with the prospective leader of the class a tentative list of questions to be considered. It was this sponsoring committee which sent out over their own names the invitations to the class. And it was this committee which saw the project through from beginning to end.

The list of questions considered is of some interest. It was decided to tackle two major topics with subquestions, as follows:

---

[16] Gleason, G., *Church Group Activities for Young Married People.* Published by the author, 1937. (The reference above is based on a digest prepared by the Bureau of Research of the International Council of Religious Education.)

1. Religious Problems in the Rearing of Children

In helping children pray should we give them set forms, or let them formulate their own prayers? Should we concentrate primarily on the saying of words, or, rather, on cultivating a feeling of readiness to pray? How early should the prayer life of children begin?

What should be the chief content of their prayers? Gratitude? Regard for others? Moral upreach? Asking for things? Is there any possibility of a child's prayer life being harmful to him?

How shall we teach children to conceive of God? How shall they think of His character? How shall they picture Him? What misconceptions of God are prevalent among children?

What sort of experience on the part of our children will mean most to their religious life? The religious example we set them? Their contact with nature? Their experience of human love?

How shall we teach children about Jesus?

How introduce them to the Bible?

What about family worship? Is it possible in our day? Is it desirable? How go at it? How make it meaningful to children?

2. The Problem of Discipline

Should we ever use corporal punishment? If so, when?

Do we as a rule punish children for their sake, or for ours?

Can punishment teach a child to be good, or merely clever?

Which is better—punishing bad behavior, or rewarding good behavior? Why?

Do we want unquestioning obedience from our children?

How important is it to develop self-reliance in our children? What bearing has this on the problem of discipline?

What bad effects of punishment may there be?

What kind of person is it who is a stern disciplinarian? How was he disciplined in his own childhood?

REACHING THE HOME

What makes some children hard to handle?
What would be our best statement of a disciplinary policy for the home?

The first evening arrived, and the parents came—about forty of them. The leader listed some of the questions on the board, opened them for discussion, and from then on made no long speeches. The mothers and fathers took the bit in their teeth and went ahead. They discussed. They argued. They reported their own experiences. They read. They thought. And they enjoyed it all thoroughly. They paid their slight registration fee without protest (this had been agreed upon primarily to give a touch of academic dignity to the venture). They entered heartily into the social hour which followed on two of the evenings. And at the end of the month they were ready to go on. (By the last evening the attendance had reached sixty.) However, it was thought best to discontinue the meetings in accordance with the original intention, and resume them later if that should seem advisable.

In retrospect, the success of this venture appears to have been due largely to the sponsorship of the committee of parents, the good fellowship which prevailed, the practical nature of the discussions, and the fact that the end of the series was clearly visible from the beginning. These would seem to be sound principles to follow in inaugurating a parents' class.

PASTORAL VISITATION AND HOME-LIFE

The old adage has it that if the mountain will not come to Mohammed, there is only one thing left for Mohammed to do—go to the mountain. There is considerable wisdom in this saying for the matter of parental education. If it is hard at times to get parents to come to the church and the minister, then let the minister go to the parents. As it happens, there is a well-established practice in the Protestant Church which takes a minister periodically into all the homes of his parish. This practice of pastoral visitation has been used in the past in the interests of the church—to tie the members more securely to the church and stimulate their attendance at its services. It has been used also in the interests of individuals—to comfort the sick, cheer the lonely, help the needy, and guide the perplexed. Why not put it to use now in the interests of the home also? As the minister stands expectantly on the doorstep, there awaits him on the inside not merely an individual or two but also a family which has a life of its own and needs of its own. Pastoral visitation is under every obligation to serve the well-being of the home.

But will the members of the home speak of their family-problems to the minister? There is an intimacy about home life which forbids too free an unveiling before an outsider. And yet, if the minister be no chance visitor to this home but a true pastor who has stood by the family's side in sickness and in health, in life and death, he is in a position to render help to the home as no one else is (with the possible exception of the doctor). To a true pastor the members of a family will speak concerning their home life. The chances of their so doing are greater if the pastor is married, has children of his own, and is favorably known as a good "family man." The chances are greater still if the pastor has fitted himself by serious study of psychology and kindred subjects to give real help to families, and has actually done so on a number of occasions. And they are increased further still if the father and mother of this home have at some time or other met with the pastor in a parents' class. A strong argument for a parents' class is its value in smoothing the way for help to individual homes as the pastor makes his round of friendly visitation.

Ideally, the parents themselves would take the initiative in a consideration of home problems with their pastor. However, it may be his privilege—and in some cases his bounden duty—to unbar the way for a discussion of some problem of the home. Even if the door between him and the home should properly be opened only from the home's side, it can at least be unlocked from his side. Sometimes the conversation can be directed tactfully and inoffensively toward the family and its individual members: "How does John like high school?" or, "I hear that Mary is getting along well in church school." The reply of the parent may be such as to throw the door open wide for serious conference concerning John and Mary. Sometimes a book or a pamphlet helps greatly to open the way. The pastor has brought it along "because I thought you might be interested in it," or "because there is a paragraph here which reminded me of your Mary," and the conversation is started. Only the pastor must avoid at all costs getting the reputation in church and community of being too solicitous about the affairs of the home. If one neighbor says to another, "Our minister is coming to see us today; I wonder what he will ask about this time!" the usefulness of that minister in those two homes is about at an end.

One clear service to be rendered the home is at the point of family worship. For various reasons this practice is having difficulty at present. The problem of time is, no doubt, a real one. The modern family finds it hard to be together at one time and in one place long enough to worship. However, it is more than likely that devout parents often fail to have family worship for the simple reason that they do not know how. It is a matter of common knowledge that the ability to lead in free prayer is becoming a lost art among Protestant laymen. And the printed materials which are offered for family worship have a habit of ignoring the children of the home. Many of them are splendid aids to mature devotion, but they seem to proceed on the assumption that the average family is made up of four or five grandparents. Thus the father of a family, or the mother, is frequently cut adrift without help either from within or from without—and the family's worship never materializes.

The minister can give such help as he makes his pastoral rounds. He can, if he so desires, recommend such a printed aid as the Children's Fellowship of Prayer booklet which was issued for the first time during the 1937 Lenten season and proved such a boon to families containing little children.[17] But he can do more; he can give help at times through his own example. Often the minister is called upon to lead the entire family in an act of worship. He might on occasion take a child's church-school quarterly as the point of departure for the worship of the entire family. Thus his own example in the home would be a sort of object lesson in the art of family worship.

Can a minister, then, leave a home with the assurance not only that these people will be in their places in church next Sunday, and that their individual lives have been touched, but also that the life of the family itself has been strengthened and enriched by his call? There is no higher mission of pastoral calling than this!

[17] *Thoughts of God for Boys and Girls*, J. Q. Miller, General Editor. The Connecticut Council of Churches and Religious Education, 1937.

Parent-Teacher Co-operation in the Church School

The modern public school makes every effort to win the intelligent support of the home. There are Parent-Teacher Associations galore throughout the land, with a national headquarters to direct and inspire the local units. And yet every reason for such co-operation that holds in the realm of the public school holds with equal or greater force in the realm of the church school. For a nonco-operative home is at least as likely to undo good teaching in religion as in arithmetic.

There are several distinct points at which parents and church-school teachers can work together to advantage. There is *the problem of attendance,* to begin with. Perhaps the only way to solve it is through school and home working hand in hand, for the church school has no truant officer; it has no compulsory church-school law; it can fall back only upon its own attractiveness and the degree to which parents catch a glimpse of its true purposes and rally to its support even at some sacrifice to their week-end plans. But this will not happen automatically! Through many a printed leaflet and many a conversation the parents must be taken on the inside of the school's life, until they see clearly what the school is trying to do and how it is trying to do it. The problem of church-school attendance will never be solved until parents are made partners in the "firm."

Again, parents and church-school teachers can work together to the great advantage of both in gaining *an understanding of the children* for whom both are concerned. They are the same children, but they react

233

differently under different personalities and in different situations. The little girl who is cowed into meek submission at home by well-meaning but thoughtless parents may blossom out into unsuspected loveliness and undreamed-of talents in the freer atmosphere of the church school. It may be a revelation to her mother and father to learn of this, and their whole treatment of her may be changed thereby. On the other hand, the little fellow who is so strangely irritable and hard to handle in church school may have suffered a long illness in his babyhood of which the teacher knows nothing. But the mother knows of it all too well! And if she is given a chance to tell the teacher this single fact, the little fellow's path in church school is suddenly made smoother and brighter. One such conversation might conceivably spell the difference between his being lost and saved to the church in later life.

Most important of all, *the church school and the home need to work together in order to give the school's teaching a reasonable chance of succeeding.* Suppose that the lesson for a given Sunday concerns prayer. A few precious moments, a story, a snatch of conversation, a brief experience with prayer itself—no more can be done in the Sunday-morning hour! Then the child returns home—but to what sort of home? To a home without private devotions, or family worship, or even grace at meals? To a home where God is never mentioned, except in an oath? To a home where prayer is mere magic and superstition? Or does he return to spend the week with a mother and father whose prayer life is reverent and intelligent, and who furthermore are aware of what the church school is at that moment trying to do and are more than anxious to co-operate to the extent of their ability? Only in the last-named home does the school have a real chance. If the church school is teaching about the Bible, the homes of the children can help immeasurably by purchasing good children's Bibles and leaving them in conspicuous places for the children to read. If the school is endeavoring to foster Christian living in any of its many phases, the several homes can undergird such teachings with what they say, and what they do, and what they understand about the manner in which life grows. Whatever the church school is attempting, it needs co-operative homes in order to make its efforts count.

It seems, then, that there is much to gain and nothing to lose from parent-teacher co-operation in the church school. The question is, How shall it be done? Much can be accomplished through printed messages describing the school's work, either carried home by the children or else sent through the mails. Some lesson materials for the children's division provide such messages ready-made. A few schools have made a beginning at preparing their own interpretations of their work. All such use of the printed page is to the good, but at best it is somewhat cold and lifeless. Parents and church-school teachers must meet one another face to face, not merely through the kind offices of their children or Uncle Sam. A great deal can be done through a visitation of the homes by the teachers—a new form of pastoral calling. Some churches set aside a week annually, usually in the early fall, for such a visitation. And then there is the simple and natural plan which the public school has used so widely but which the church school has rarely attempted—a Parent-Teacher Meeting. But, some cynic will say, will the parents come to such a meeting? As it happens, the cynic is right; they will not come in great numbers, especially at first. Perhaps we cannot hope for parents to attend a meeting of this sort so long as the church school is taken so lightly by everyone. Why should they give up an evening in the interests of a work which is run haphazardly, and stands no great chance of succeeding at any rate? As the church school takes itself more seriously, a parent-teacher meeting will seem less incongruous than at present and will be more likely to win a good attendance. It is instructive in this connection to note the pressure which is brought to bear upon the parents of the children in what is reputed to be the finest church school in America. A parent would scarcely think of declining to attend the quarterly parent-teacher meetings of this school.[18]

Let us not, then, despair too soon! As our church schools improve, the parents may be expected to take a livelier interest in them. And as parents concern themselves more and more with our church schools, they are bound to grow rapidly in Christian effectiveness.

YOUNG PEOPLE AND TOMORROW'S HOMES

The whole parent education movement has been in some danger of offering splendid training about five or ten years too late. We would not wait to train ministers or doctors until they were in the thick of their responsibilities. We would be horror-stricken by the vision of what might happen to churches and to invalids while the ministers and doctors were mastering their trades. And yet this is precisely what we have done in large measure in the parent education move-

[18] *The Christian Century*, February 27, 1935, pp. 269ff. "The Real Thing in Religious Education," by M. H. Bro.

ment. We have waited until people were actually parents to begin their parental training.

This is unsatisfactory from almost every possible point of view. As it happens, some of the hardest adjustments which a married couple will ever have to make fall within the first year or even the first month of their life together. Similarly, in the rearing of children it is the first three years which count most heavily. If help is to be given at all, part of it at least ought to come prior to those first three years. Besides, people do not suddenly become either good or bad homemakers when the marriage ceremony is performed, nor yet when their first child is born. We need to find ways of starting to train for Christian home life long before the home is actually established.

It is heartening to note how seriously young people will respond to an opportunity to discuss both present and future problems which have to do with Christian home life. We might suppose that they would merely snicker self-consciously and make a farce of the whole matter, but this is not usually the case. It does the heart good, for example, to recall a discussion on this topic in a week-end youth conference wherein a young engaged couple sat unashamed in the front row and listened eagerly to all that was said. Or consider the following set of topics which was announced on a printed folder for a series of Sunday-evening meetings by a typical young people's group:

"GIRL-BOY RELATIONS"

What is the Christian answer to these problems?
March 7 and 14—"Dating"
1. How old should I be before beginning to date? Why?
2. What requirements should I prefer of the person who is to be my date?

3. Should I blind date?
4. What ideals of behavior should I uphold on my date? Will high ideals have a tendency to make me a back number?
5. Should a boy (or girl) of one social standing date a person of a different social standing?
6. How far can differences of religion (Catholic vs. Hebrew vs. Protestant) serve to make unhappy a girl and boy relation?
   a. Do differences in financial standing offer the same danger?
   b. Differences in education? in personality? in culture? in age?

April 4 and 11—"On What Basis Should I Choose My Home Partner?"

1. How much should parents have to say in their children's choosing a life-mate?
2. Is it possible for two people closely associated daily with each other (e.g., in an office, in classrooms, etc.) to believe they love each other when in reality they do not?
3. To what degree should they have common interests?
4. What questions should be definitely settled before an engagement between the two is entered into?
5. What is the value of long and short engagements respectively?
6. Should there be an equality of responsibilities (financial, especially) between the two?
7. How should they treat each other during the period of going together?

April 25 and May 2—"How Can We Best Insure a Christian and Happy Home Life?"

1. At what age should young people marry?
2. Should the wife continue to work? Should she follow a profession?
3. Should the financial responsibilities for the conduct of the home be the man's own, or should they be borne by both husband and wife?

4. Should the newly married live with the parents-in-law?
5. What are the most likely causes of trouble between husband and wife?
6. What place has religion in the life of the home? Is church attendance necessary?
7. What is the real and true meaning of our marriage ceremonies and marriage vows?

If questions such as these can be handled wisely, wholesomely, and under mature leadership, it is easy to see how many a heartache for both parents and children may be averted in later years.

To the public meeting there must be added the individual conference, for there are some matters which lend themselves only to private conference. An amazing story is that of a minister who said it was customary in his congregation for young people contemplating marriage to drop in casually at his home some time before the ceremony. They came singly—the boy one evening, and the girl another—and the pastor talked with them about the new relationship they were on the verge of entering. This minister reported that to the best of his knowledge no marriage which he had solemnized had ever ended in divorce. In truth, the individual and the group methods supplement each other nicely. Each can do something which the other cannot; and each is invaluable to a happy Christian home life.

In Conclusion

An almost incredible set of statistics is that compiled by Doctor Fiske on the basis of a study which he himself made.[19] The data concern 22,001 church-

[19] Fiske, George Walter, *The Changing Family*. Harper & Brothers, 1928, p. 206.

going white families from 61 parishes in 15 states. The histories of these families were in each case secured from pastors who had been personally acquainted with them over a period of years. It will be noted that these were not American families chosen at random; they were all families which were rather closely and consistently affiliated with the Christian Church. In this whole number there were only 196 divorces—less than 1 in 100. The full force of this fact breaks upon us when we compare it with the ratio which prevailed among American families generally (at the time Doctor Fiske's book was written that ratio was 1 in 7).

The chances are that these figures prove somewhat less than they seem to prove, but even after all discounts and explanations have been made, they still stand unshaken as an eloquent witness to the worth of Christianity and the church in everyday living. They seem to say clearly that religion helps to hold a home together. They seem to say also that affiliation with the church helps to hold a home together.

It does seem as though the family and the Christian religion were meant for one another. The connection between the two is not casual and superficial but deep-lying and fundamental. It is no accident that Jesus used the language of the family to describe the kingdom of God—Father, brothers, love, sacrifice. For the family is the prototype of the Kingdom-ideal; it is also one of the cells for the building of the Kingdom in actuality. The family and the Christian religion, then, belong together naturally. If they are separated, both lose heavily. They must at all costs be kept united. "What therefore God hath joined together, let not man put asunder."

X

CHRISTIAN EDUCATION IN STRANGE PLACES

Time and again people have missed a great blessing by looking too steadily in the wrong direction. Great personages as well as great benefits to humanity frequently come over the horizon in unexpected and unconventional places. In the days of the prophet Amos people looked for real religion either in the priests with their endless round of services, or else in the school of the prophets. Those were, as everyone knew, the quarters where religion was to be found. The last place where they expected to discover it was in the personage of a shepherd and dresser of sycomore trees who came out of nowhere, delivered his fiery and unwelcome message, and departed into the wilderness again. And so they missed the voice of God! It has been true in every day that vital religion and vital education often spring up in strange places.

It behooves us, therefore, not to get straitjacketed in our thinking about Christian education. The spirit of man is not limited to a few conventional channels; neither is the Spirit of God. The means of grace are many and varied. True Christian education not uncommonly crops out in strange places.

The Grinding Wheels of Church Organization

This is, by all odds, the strangest of all strange places in which to hope to find any growth of Christian personality. We usually have little but contempt for

241

church organization and administration, and our attitude has not been helped a great deal by the prophet Ezekiel's invention of that glorious phrase, "a wheel within a wheel." These words seem to describe all too well the lifeless grinding of church machinery. But the wheels of church organization—like all other wheels—can either grind and crush, or they can be made to turn for the good of mankind.

There are two ways in which we may think of any organization—a woman's missionary society, for example. We may, in the first place, regard it merely as a means of getting something done. A certain amount of money must be raised, perhaps, for a chapel in India, and the society exists to raise the money. In this case the reason for the society's existence lies beyond it. But, secondly, we may regard any organization as an educational device. The members of the society and their spiritual growth—these too are worth considering. In this latter way of thinking the reason for the society's existence is to be found within its own membership.

These two ways of viewing an organization stress, respectively, the *objective* and the *subjective* values. In all probability we have thought of organization too much in terms of the former, to the neglect of the latter. The extreme example, of course, is an army. An army exists to accomplish a military objective—the taking of Hill 29, for instance. What happens meanwhile to those in the organization—their bodies, their morals, their initiative, their freedom, their ideals—is wholly secondary. In such a case the subjective values are almost completely subordinated to the objective. In ordinary life we do not go quite so far, but often too far. We need, therefore, to think carefully upon the ways in which organization—even organization!—can be made to promote the spiritual growth of persons.

As a matter of fact, *there is scarcely a single aspect of Christian personality which cannot be sought within the grinding wheels of church organization,* if they be made to turn aright. Almost any objective that can be achieved through talking to people can be achieved also through catching them up in proper forms of organization. Is it a devotion to the kingdom of God which we should like to cultivate in people's hearts? We might, of course, preach a sermon to them on the stirring text, "Seek ye first the kingdom of God," and that would be worth while. But the same end could be sought and achieved through engaging these same people in real efforts to usher in God's kingdom on earth. If they actually turn their hands to the furtherance of world peace, or the elimination of vicious movies, and experience firsthand the thrill of enlisting in a great cause, they may emerge from the experience with a devotion to the Kingdom that no volume of words could engender. But this is a matter of committees, subcommittees, and officers—in other words, of organization. Or, is it a sense of responsibility which we would like to nurture in our young people? We might, conceivably, plan a lesson period on this topic, with proper analysis of what we mean by responsibility and many illustrations drawn from life. That would be worth while. But we might also entrust to a harum-scarum group of high-school boys and girls some real responsibility for the conduct of a congregational social, which would sober them and mature them and prepare them for greater faithfulness in the future. But this too is a matter of organization and administration.

Even the deeper personality needs of individual persons can be met through these same despised channels. Here is a young girl who is shy, self-conscious, overly dependent upon others, mistrustful of her own ability. Can we do anything, through organization, to expand her shrunken personality? Of course we can! We can begin by assigning her a minor rôle on a worship committee; then a major rôle; then, perhaps, the position of pianist. As she goes from stage to stage, her sense of self-reliance and competency grows apace. It is possible for her to become a new person through a wise and humane policy of administration. And here is her exact opposite, a young man cocksure of himself, used to the spotlight, self-consciously good and capable—a Pharisee if ever there were one! What can we do for him? We can give him the experience of laboring hard for a dramatic production but always behind the scenes, working hour after hour with not even his name appearing in the final program. This may be a means of grace to his soul, and it too is a matter of organization.

In short, church machinery can be run not only for the good the person can do the cause, but also for the good the cause can do the person. But to view organization thus is to transfigure it. It becomes alive and full of human interest. It is redeemed from the disrepute into which it has fallen, and made a significant phase of Christian education.

THE OFFERING

We hear much in some quarters nowadays about stewardship education. There are essay contests, courses of study, books of stories—all calculated to teach Christian stewardship. Without reflecting upon the value of these methods, we may still say truthfully that the supreme moment for stewardship education arrives when the minister makes that momentous announcement, "Our morning offering will now be received." Let us suppose that in that moment an adolescent boy reaches into his pocket for a nickel which his father gave him before leaving home for church, and deposits it in the collection plate with no clear-cut idea of what is to become of it. That represents about as mechanical a process as could well be imagined. An inventive genius could probably devise a machine to perform this operation flawlessly. It is transacted purely on the muscular level. Neither the heart nor the mind of the boy is called into play as the nickel makes its precarious way from the father's pocket to the church collection plate. At all events, if we allow such thoughtless and heartless offerings on the part of this boy for twenty years, it is no mystery if he fails to support the church adequately in the years of his manhood.

By way of contrast, consider the way in which one church school handles the matter of its offerings, at least during certain seasons of the year. During the four Sundays before Christmas and the six Sundays before Easter this school receives special offerings which are remarkable on several counts. In the first place, the pupils have a clear notion where these offerings go. The Lenten fund is always devoted to the cause of missions. The pre-Christmas offering is used in the beautifying of the church sanctuary, and the pupils themselves have practically the final word in deciding what project shall be chosen each year. In the second place, no pupil is allowed to contribute a cent during these periods which he has not earned by his own effort. The pastor of the church has kept a record over the years of the diverse ways in which the members of the school have earned the money for their offerings, and the list now reaches the astounding total of 381 different ways. It is perhaps not irrelevant to add that about 250 pupils, mostly children and young people in moderate circumstances, give about $1,000 each year in these two special offerings.

There appear to be, then, two chief conditions which must be met if the giving of money is to be educational and spiritually uplifting. These two conditions have to do with the "whence" and the "whither" of the money. The first is that the giver should not come by his money too easily. It ought to involve some sacrifice on his part, at least some outlay of effort. And the second is that the giver be intelligent about the destination of his gift, and preferably have a share in choosing that destination himself.

This second condition leads us squarely into the making of a protest—a protest against our present lifeless manner of handling church benevolences. A giver nowadays is so far removed from the final destination of his gift that he often knows little about that destination and cares less. Mr. Average Church-Member in America is not challenged to give his hard-earned money for the support of a particular kindergarten in Japan, or hospital in India. There would be something real and soul-stirring about such giving! Instead his denomination lumps together all its kindergartens in Japan, hospitals in India, colleges everywhere, struggling home-mission congregations in America, promotional expenses for Christian education, orphans, aged ministers, and perhaps throws in a sum for the Federal Council of the Churches of

Christ in America. This grand total is then divided by the number of active members in the denomination, and each member's share comes down to him as an "apportionment" or something equally lifeless.

We must not close our eyes to the real difficulties which beset any other plan than the one now in vogue. However, some denominations have made a beginning. They specify definite benevolent "objects" which congregations or individuals can accept as their own. If an "object" is too large—a hospital, for example, or a college—they chop it up into beds or scholarships or even small units called "shares," so that even the small giver can lay hold of something tangible and specific. This is a step in the right direction. Can we go farther, and put practically all of our benevolent giving on such a basis? The additional money received and the new interest created might more than pay for the extra secretaries required to keep the lines open between giver and receiver. At the very least, the matter deserves careful thought and some honest experimentation.

After the denomination has perfected its machinery, there still remains much for the local church to do in order that the giving of money may be good for the soul of the giver. It must exhaust all the available ways—charts, posters, motion pictures, visits of missionaries, and so forth—for portraying vividly to young and old what becomes of moneys after they leave the collection plate. It must also study how to give even children and young people a proper share in determining where their offerings shall go. To this end an occasional church-school assembly, or a meeting of representatives of the several classes and groups, is very much in order.

Thus in due time we shall rescue the offering from the evils that so often attend it. It will cease to be a mere routine, or a time for idle gossip, or an occasion for special pleading and the employment of contests and schemes of dubious sorts. Instead, it will rise to the level of an intelligent and hearty outpouring of financial substance on behalf of great causes. In such a context the giving of money becomes true Christian education.

CLEANSING THE COMMUNITY

If any defense were needed for including such a heading in a treatment of Christian education, it could be made along familiar lines. A church can preach and teach its heart out in a letter-perfect program of Christian education, and all its efforts will count for nothing if the environing community drags down as fast as the church lifts up. After the hour or two hours spent weekly in the church, then what? The young people, especially, sally forth from the church doors into a truly diabolic conglomeration of roadhouses, burlesque shows, sex and crime motion pictures, gambling pools and devices of every description, salacious pulp magazines, houses of prostitution, and other evil inventions too numerous to mention. We of the church sometimes bury our heads, ostrich-like, beneath a mass of rationalizations so that we may not have to see and deal with these things. We say that the picture is greatly overdrawn; whereas in truth it is commonly underdrawn. Who would suspect, for example, that there are about 400 pulp magazines in America reaching from 15 to 30 million readers? (About 100 of the worst of these are banned entirely from Canada.) Or, we say that these evil influences do of course prevail in certain metropolitan areas, but that our own communities are in large measure untouched by them; whereas there is no community in America into which they do not penetrate. To continue the pulp magazines as a single example of a general truth, an observer saw a huge stack of these magazines unloaded in a village drugstore one day—only to disappear, as if by magic, by the next day. On any given Sunday morning it is impossible for a pastor to know what his young people have been through during the past week, unless he has made a complete investigation—and if he is not willing to be shocked he had better not make the investigation!

These evil influences are real, they are well-nigh universal, and they are truly devilish. To cleanse a community of them becomes a legitimate and essential part of a full-blown program of Christian education.

Consider, for example, what was actually accomplished in one city in the course of a year. Is this worth while? Is this entitled to be called Christian education?

October, 1934

Reported 17 claw-gambling machines to the chief of police, who had them suppressed.

Reported also 1 gambling wheel and 4 gambling games, which were stopped.

Reported a writer of obscene letters, who was afterward arrested.

December, 1934

Advised against a "Walkathon" at a near-by park, which was afterward suppressed by the State Department of Labor and Industry through the county's district attorney.

Prevented a "Bingo" gambling party through the chief of police.

Had the *National Police Gazette* suppressed through the district attorney's office.

Complaints brought against the proprietor of the Central Hotel and 2 women frequenters. They were prosecuted by the mayor and police and jailed by the court.

Indecent dancing stage show stopped at motion-picture theater.

January, 1935

Indecent burlesque stage show at another theater stopped, and the proprietor warned by the chief of police.

Motion-picture theater stage shows kept under surveillance throughout the year, 36 visits being made.

February, 1935

Protests sent to members of the state legislature against race-track gambling bills. An open letter on the evils of race-track gambling published in the newspapers of the community.

May, 1935

Reported an Italian lottery in the city with a top prize of $1,000,000. The agent arrested by the police.

Ballyhoo magazine resuppressed through the district attorney's office.

Big one-night girl tent show—attended by 1,200 people, mostly young people—kept within bounds.

Automobile lottery driven from the city through a complaint to the mayor.

Medicine-show lottery stopped.

June, July, August, 1935

Sideshows of all circuses visiting the community kept clean.

Proprietresses of 4 vice resorts reported to the mayor and chief of police. They were successfully prosecuted and convicted.

Work such as this in the direction of a community wherein children have a chance to grow up clean cannot be done by one man, nor by one church. In the above-mentioned case the moving force was an organization called a Law and Order Society, whose spearhead is a small directing group numbering about twenty public-spirited citizens. During a quarter of a century it has unceasingly fought a good fight on the side of decency.

A development of great promise has taken place recently in Los Angeles County, California, which may point the way to a helpful plan of attack upon community sore spots. In the attempt to cope with the problem of delinquency, this county has set up half a hundred organizations called Co-ordinating Councils in as many separate localities—the purpose of each Council being to tie together into one effective unit all community agencies which are concerned with human welfare. The plan of organization for each Council includes a committee whose name, membership, and function are of especial interest in this connection. The committee's name is "The Environment Committee." Its membership includes representatives of such institutions as churches, schools, Parent-Teacher Associations, service clubs, women's clubs, and the American Legion. Its function is, in part, to assemble information concerning motion-picture theaters, pool halls, dance halls, beer halls, gambling, salacious magazines and books, advertising, and radio programs, and to put all such information together with plans for positive action into the hands of the proper authorities.[1] Here is a lead which countless communities throughout the nation might do well to follow.

---

[1] Scudder, K. J., and Beam, K. S., *Who Is Delinquent?* Rotary Club of Los Angeles, 1934, pp. 45f.

Such work surely is Christian education—on its preventive side. In a certain children's hospital there is a department which goes by the magical name of D.P.D.—"The Department for the Prevention of Disease." Such a department is long overdue in the program of Christian education—a department for the prevention of moral disease. If it is legitimate to save a boy from ruin by a discussion of life-situations and moral standards, it is just as legitimate and perhaps a little surer to accomplish the same result by removing some of the moral pitfalls from his way.

SERVICE TO INDIVIDUALS, INSTITUTIONS, CAUSES

There is nothing better for the soul than to be of service, whether to needy individuals, needy institutions, or needy causes. Doctor Cabot, who has shown so much true discernment of what men live by and for, has packed a wealth of wisdom into a stray sentence in one of his writings: "At our best we escape into a wholehearted deed." He might have added that we *become* our best by escaping frequently into wholehearted deeds.

It seems unthinkable that Christians should have neglected so largely this avenue of Christian growth, because it belongs so unmistakably to the genius of Christianity. If there is any one characteristically Christian strategy of personality-growth, this is it! Was it not Jesus who said, "He that loseth his life for my sake shall find it"? Time and again in the New Testament this same teaching appears. The later ages of Christian history have verified it, and modern psychology now confirms it. From every standpoint it is clear that the best way of growth toward the "measure of the stature of the fullness of Christ" is not to think about it overmuch, but, rather, to lose oneself in something outside oneself a hundred times larger than oneself. And yet many a boy has gone through ten years of church school and church without once being given an opportunity to "escape into a wholehearted deed." All too often we say to him, in effect: "Now sit down, talk and be talked to, pray and be prayed about; we shall open to you every avenue of Christian growth except the real one of losing your life for the kingdom of God." The boy talks, and prays, and sings, and occasionally gives out the hymnals—and wonders why the Christian life is so dull and uninteresting, and what is meant by the strange talk in the New Testament of joy, and peace, and an abundant life. He has experienced nothing of the sort! Yet all the while there lies about him on every side a world fairly crying out for the investment of every talent he possesses. A world in dire need of wholehearted deeds, and a boy whose whole being is struggling for escape into such deeds— and never do the twain meet! *Herein lies the greatest present weakness in Christian education!*

The difficulties in the way of remedying this defect are undeniably real. We know so little about a realistic program of service in the local church. We know a good deal about talking, and singing, and praying in the church program. There are books a-plenty on all these topics, and professors at our theological seminaries, and well-established bodies of knowledge. But when it comes to doing and serving we are at a loss. The average professor of Christian education can teach learnedly about the technique of the discussion method or the construction of a worship service, but when the subject of a realistic program of Christian service is raised, he lapses into an eloquent silence.

But our failure is not due altogether to our lack of knowledge. The sad truth is that this is a field into which we do not really want to enter. It is so much easier to plan beautiful services of worship and nicely wrought-out recreational programs than to go to the help of needy families, or to break a lance in the cause of international peace. But these difficulties are not insurmountable. They will most surely fall before a proper array of ingenuity, courage, Christian love, and hard work.

As proof that such is the case, we may cite the experience of a typical church school in a village community. The pastor of this church realized that the service phase of his school's program was being neglected. Accordingly, he set as his goal the enlistment of each class in at least two enterprises of actual Christian service during the year 1936. First the officers and teachers of the school discussed the matter back and forth, and agreed to make the attempt. Then it was laid before the entire school for adoption. The pastor held himself responsible for suggesting projects from time to time, and the several classes took hold with an eagerness which they had not dared hope for. A partial record of the service projects completed by this average school in about a year's time is as follows:

Children brought fruit at Thanksgiving time, arranged it in the church for the worship service, and later distributed it to children in hospitals.

Children held a Christmas service with an offering for a denominational orphanage. They brought gifts and placed them under the tree, and encouraged the congregation to add their gifts for the orphans.

Junior girls selected books from the Sunday-school library, cleaned and repaired them when necessary, and sent them to the Philippines for educational work.

Junior girls gathered appropriate used Christmas cards, mounted them, and sent them to Japan for missionary use.

Intermediates arranged for, planned, and conducted a service in a near-by home for the aged.

Intermediates selected an item of the congregational apportionment which had to do with a denominational home for the aged, sold candy to raise the necessary amount, and made a study of the work of the home.

Three boys' groups combined to plan, install, and pay for a buzzer system for the Sunday school.

A young ladies' class visited every family in the congregation quarterly in the interest of the church-building fund.

A group of women went to a near-by hospital to do necessary sewing. They enlisted a number of other women in the community in this project.

A women's class made a quilt for a denominational orphanage.

In connection with the renovation of the parsonage several groups selected items for which they assumed responsibility—window shades, linoleum, paint, etc.

The boys sponsored a Father-and-Son Banquet for the community.

A young ladies' class sponsored a Mother-and-Daughter Banquet for the community.

A young ladies' class planned an evening of pictures and music for the community.

An adult group investigated available materials on courtship, family life, etc., and purchased a number of them for the use of the young people.

This does not pretend to be an ideal service program. It includes nothing spectacular. Perhaps its greatest weakness lies in the fact that it passed by entirely the whole realm of major social issues. But it does represent an honest attempt on the part of a whole church school to go beyond mere talk and channel a part of its energies into actual Christian service.

What this church did any church can do. The precise manner in which it is to be done will, of course, vary greatly from place to place. It is essential that someone in the congregation—the pastor, perhaps, or else a committee—be on the lookout for individuals, institutions, and causes which need the help of Christian people. The need should be absolutely genuine, for trumped-up projects of service are worse, if anything, than none at all. These opportunities can then be referred to the groups best fitted to take them up. Some church schools regularly invite community and denominational agencies—the Red Cross, Community Chest, orphanages, hospitals, peace societies, denominational boards, et cetera—to appear before them on behalf of their respective causes. When the world's needs have been brought vividly to the attention of the school or congregation, the task is half done—but only half! It remains to cultivate in the workers of the school or church a keen sense of the value of service-projects, and a growing ability to handle them well. And—after the workers—the official board may well consider thoughtfully the place of service in the Christian life and the Christian church. Finally, the time is ripe for projecting a program of service for an entire congregation which shall be as thoroughgoing as the program of study or of worship.

There are sound reasons for believing that here lies the next great step in Christian education. We can go little farther in the refinement of the discussion method, or the technique of worship, or even individual counseling. There may, of course, be revolutionary developments in all these fields just over the horizon, but at present there are no intimations of them. On the contrary, we can go a great deal farther in developing a realistic program of Christian service to individuals, institutions, and causes, because we have barely started. It seems, then, that the next great step in Christian education is to conceive of our churches as workshops—actual workshops—for the kingdom of God.

If work for the Kingdom becomes truly central, all other phases of the church's program are more than likely to take care of themselves. If we work sufficiently hard for the Kingdom, we shall study—we shall have to! We shall be driven to it by the greatness of the task and our own ignorance. If we work sufficiently hard for the Kingdom, we shall worship—we shall have to! We shall be driven to it by the magnitude of the task and our own littleness. And if we work sufficiently hard for the Kingdom, we shall fellowship—we shall have to! We shall know the high fellowship which comes from traveling the same road together and sharing the same burden. May it be, by any chance, that there is a special meaning for Christian educators in the age-old promise: "But seek ye first his kingdom, and his righteousness; and all these things shall be added unto you"?